Adult Coloring Book For Men

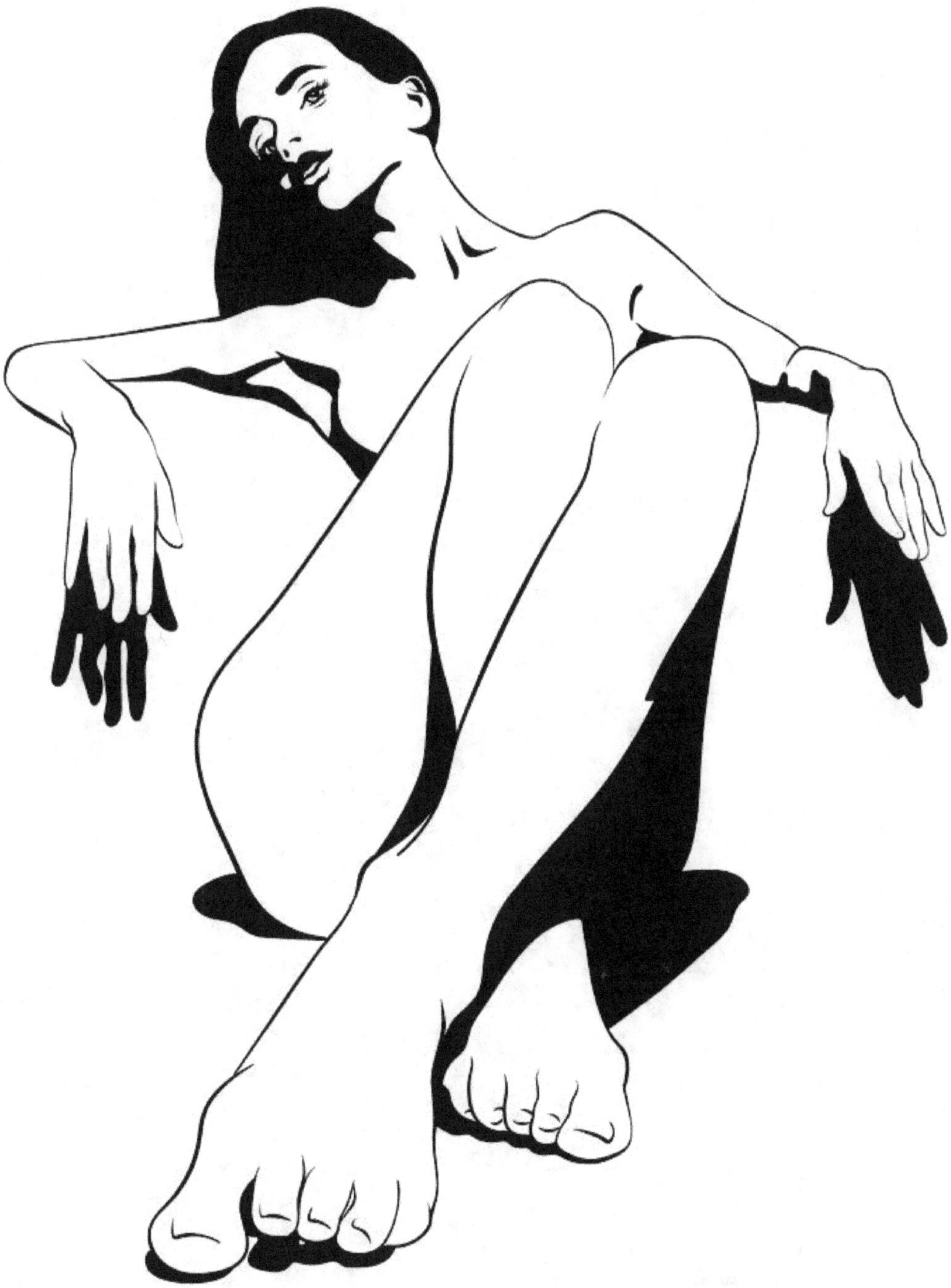

Copyright © 2020 Katrin Stark

ALL RIGHTS RESERVED

COLOR TEST PAGE

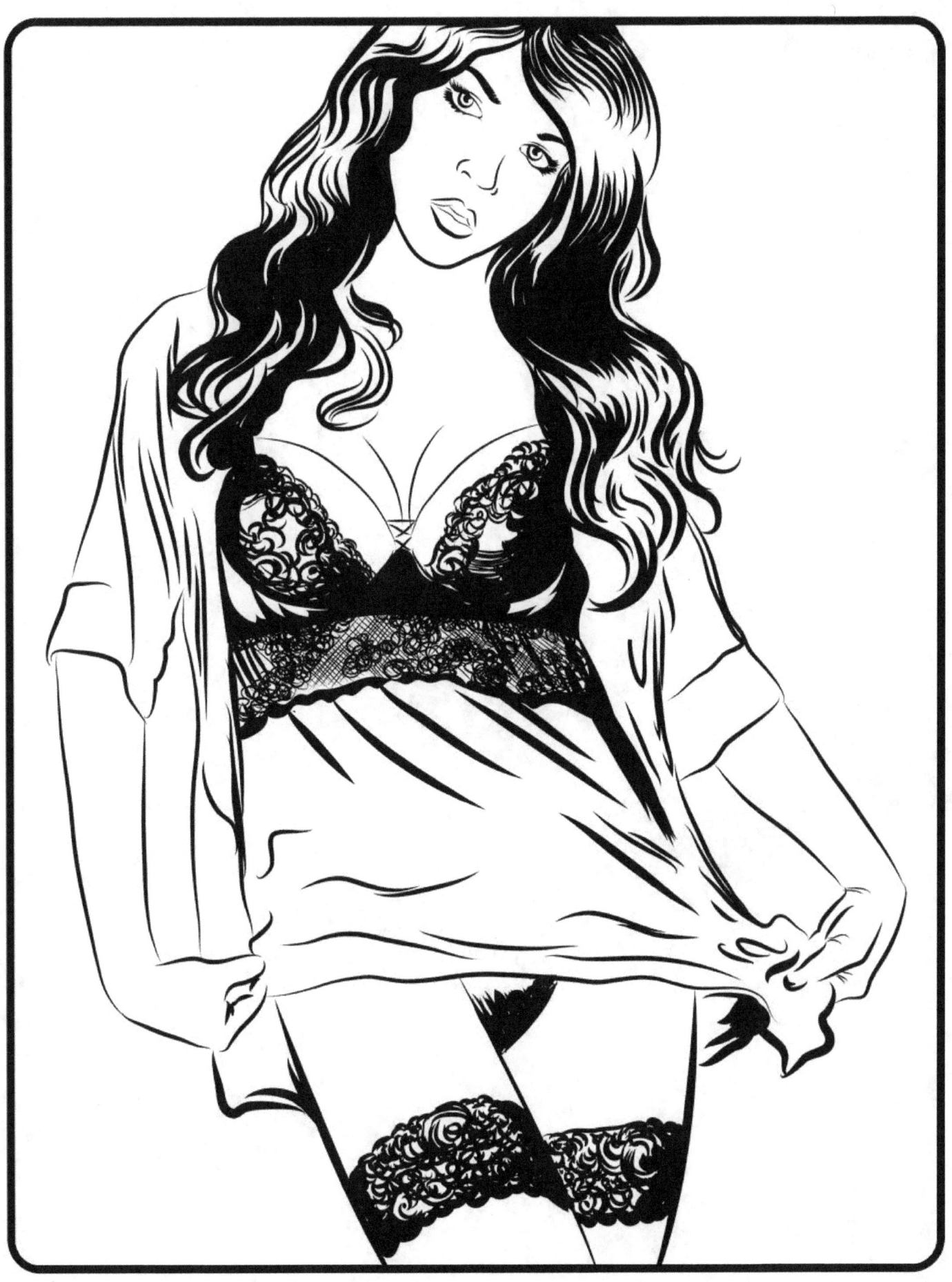

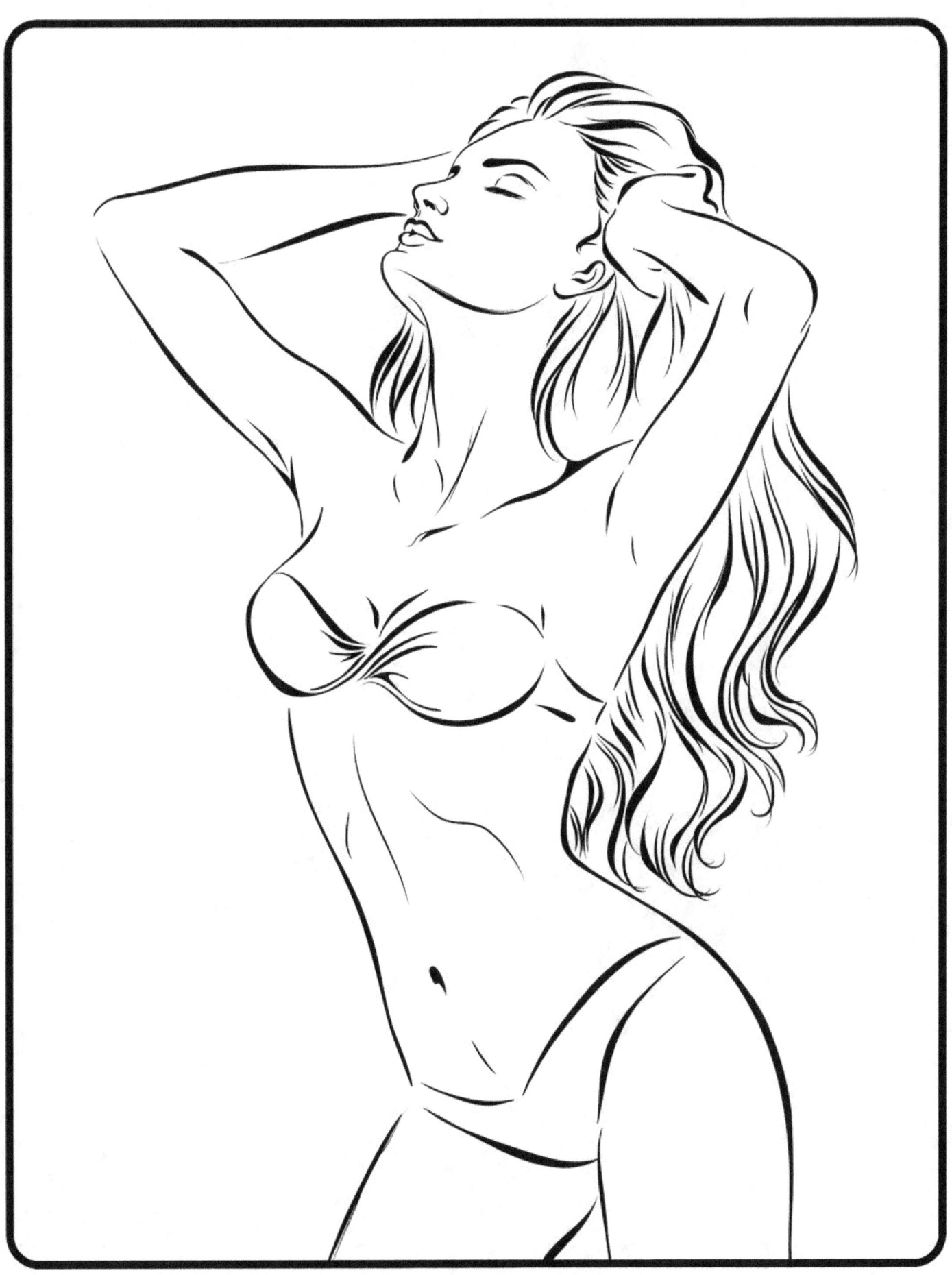

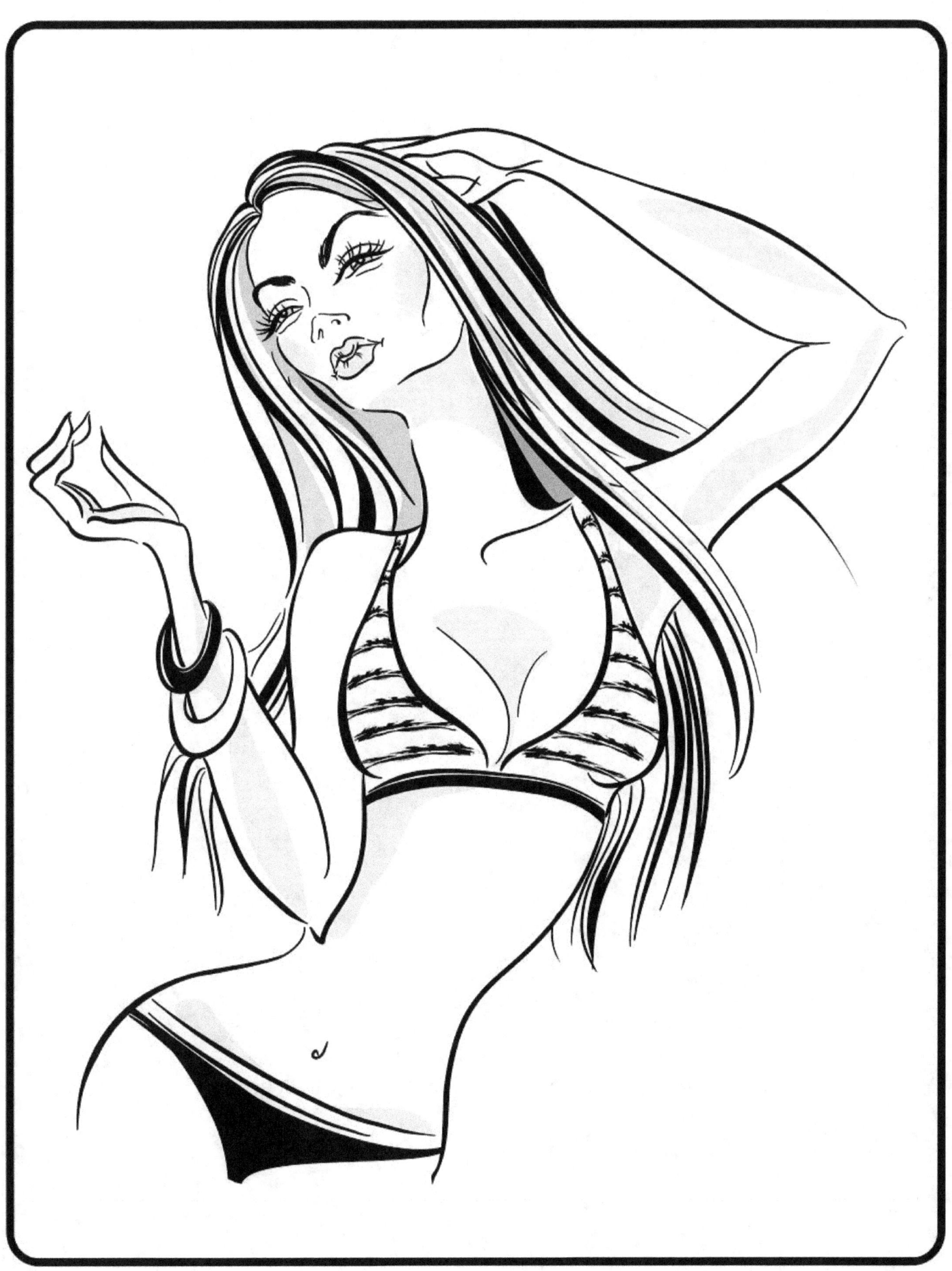

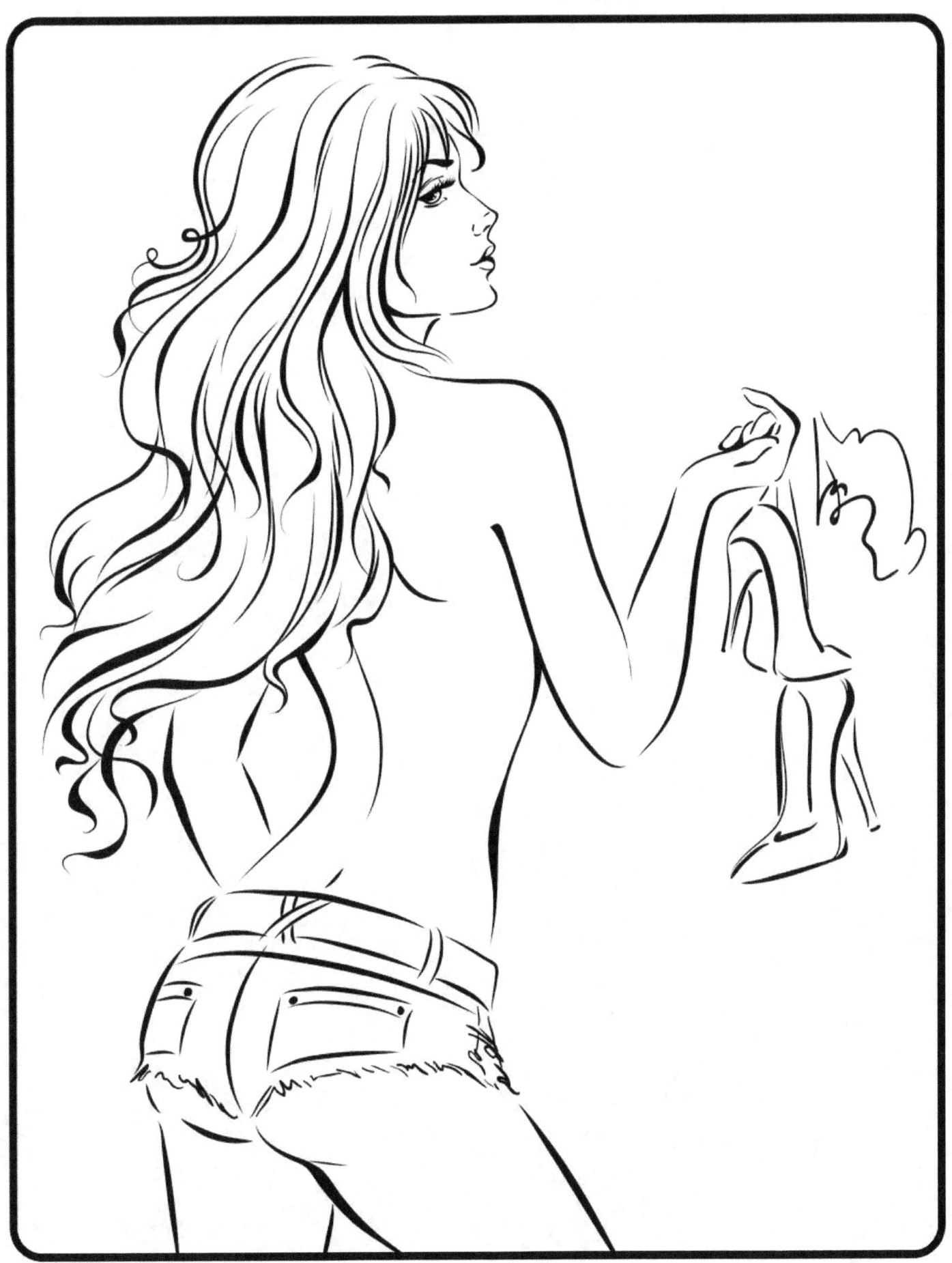

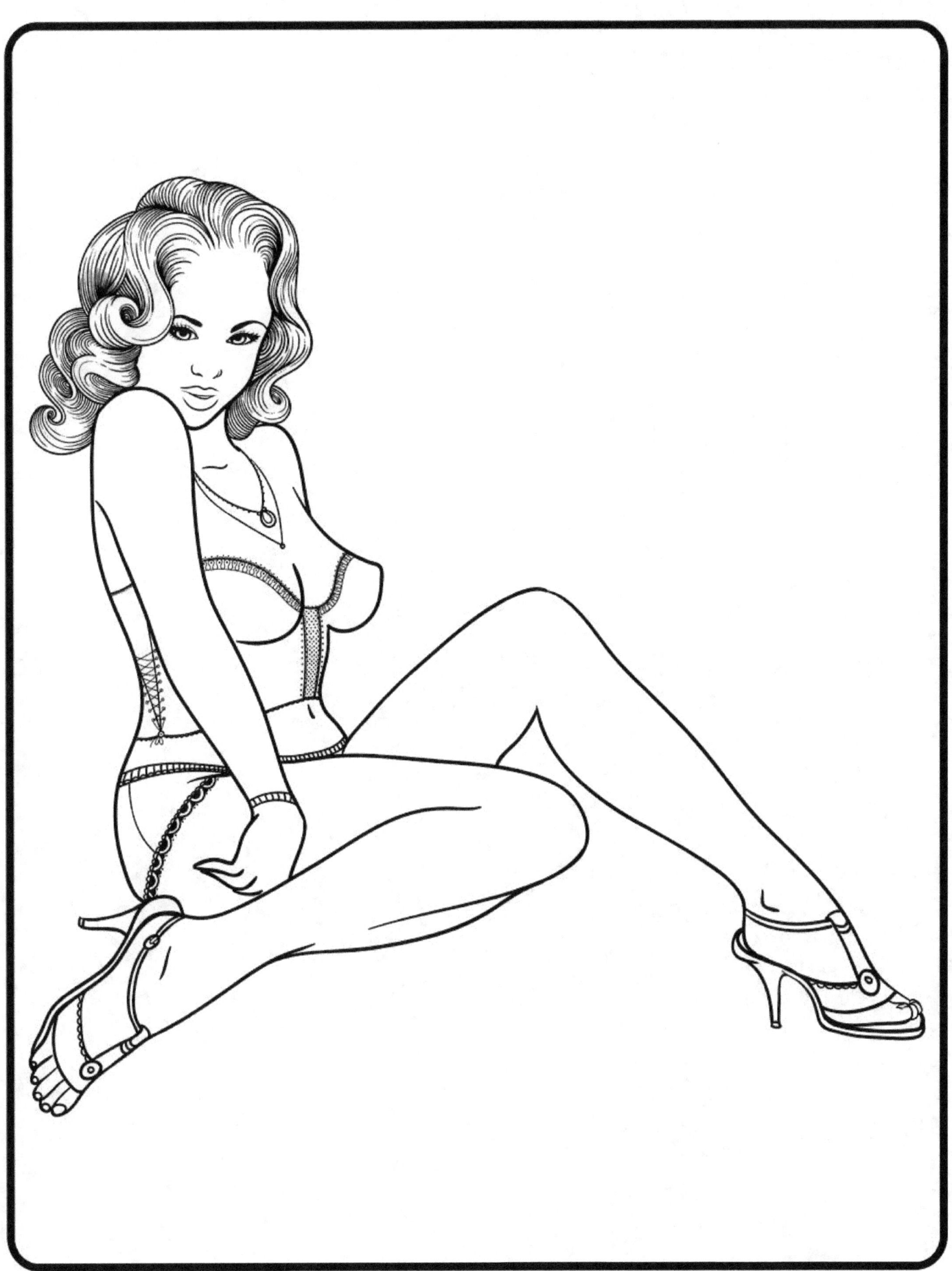

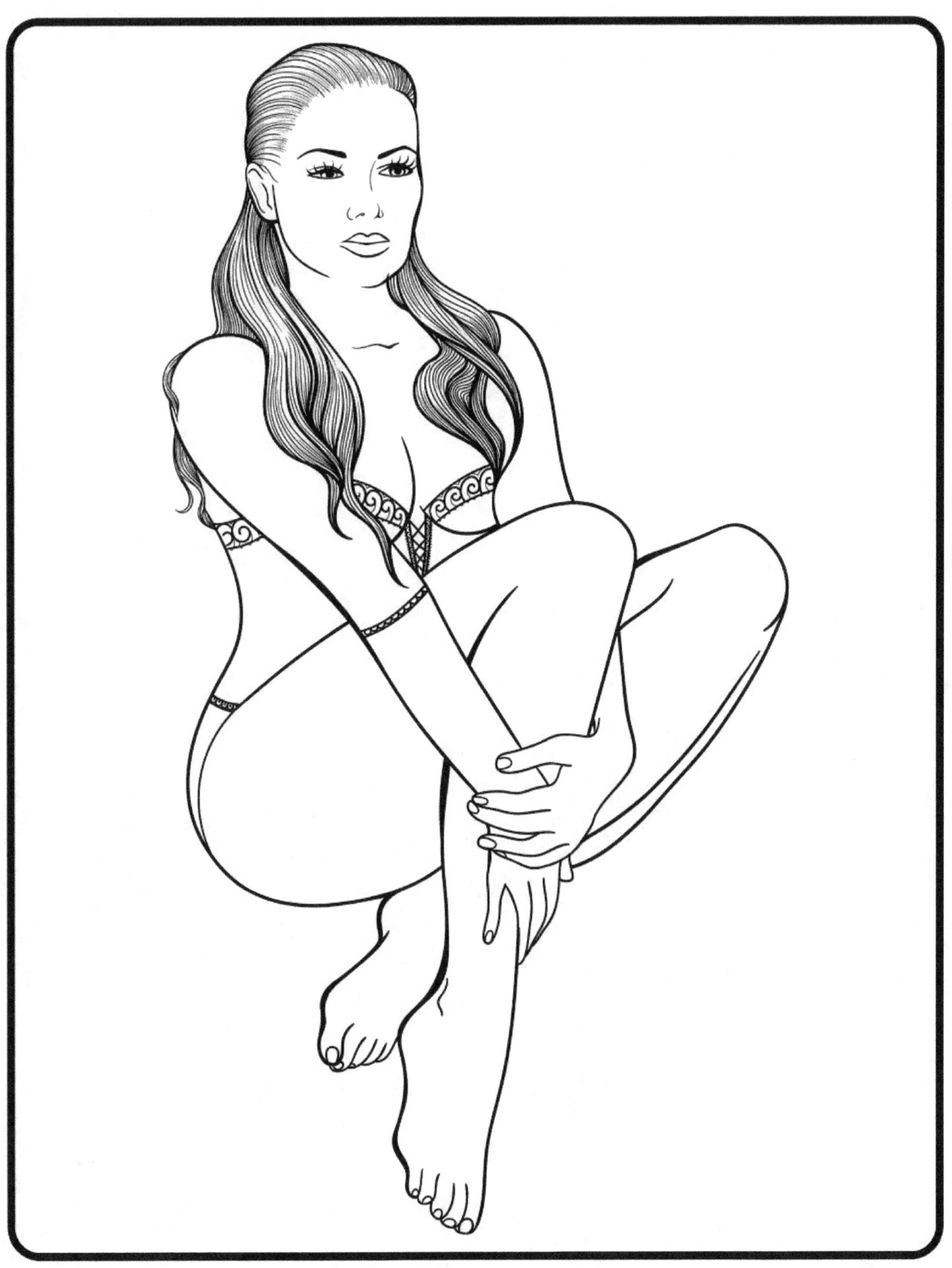

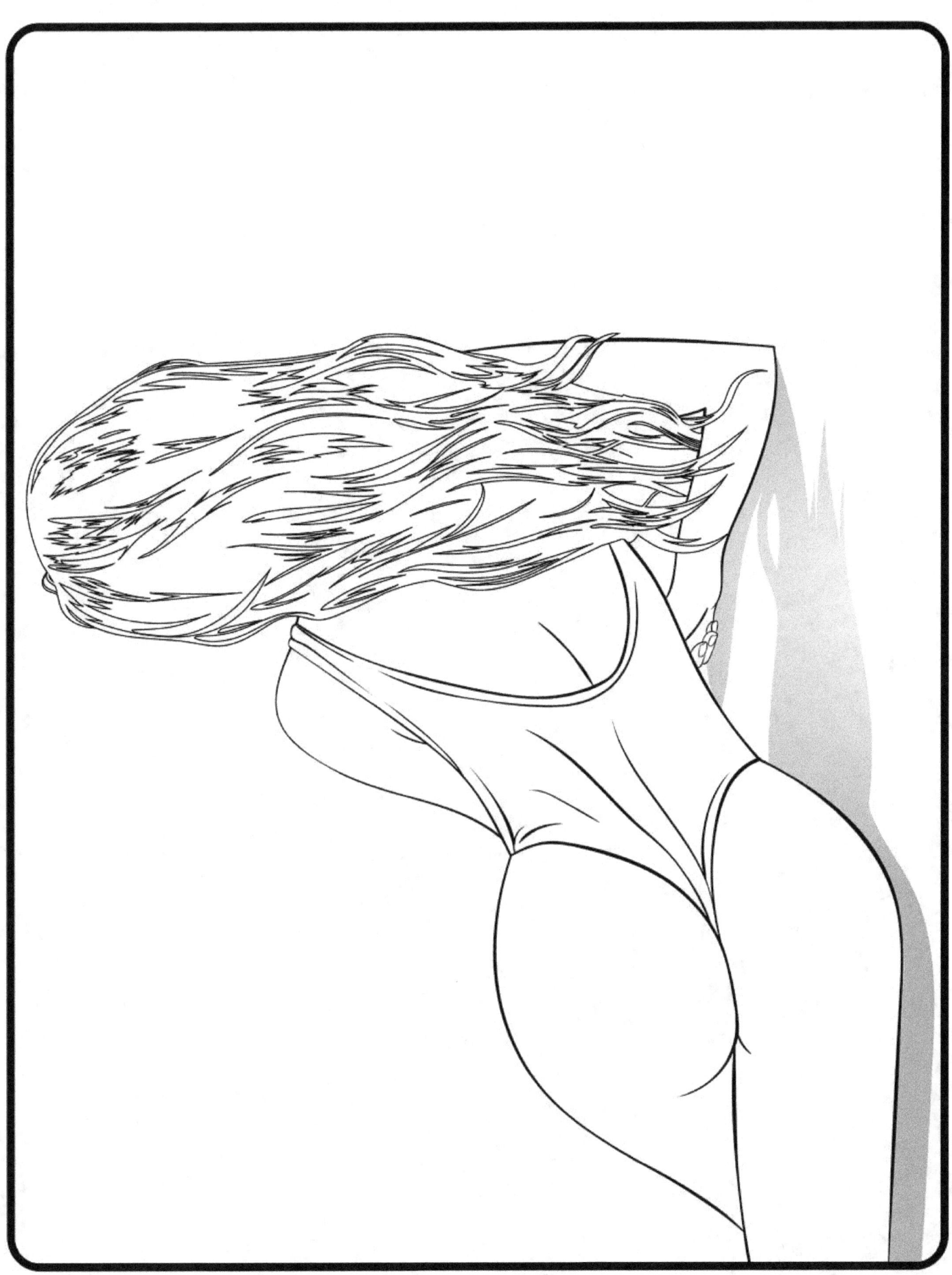

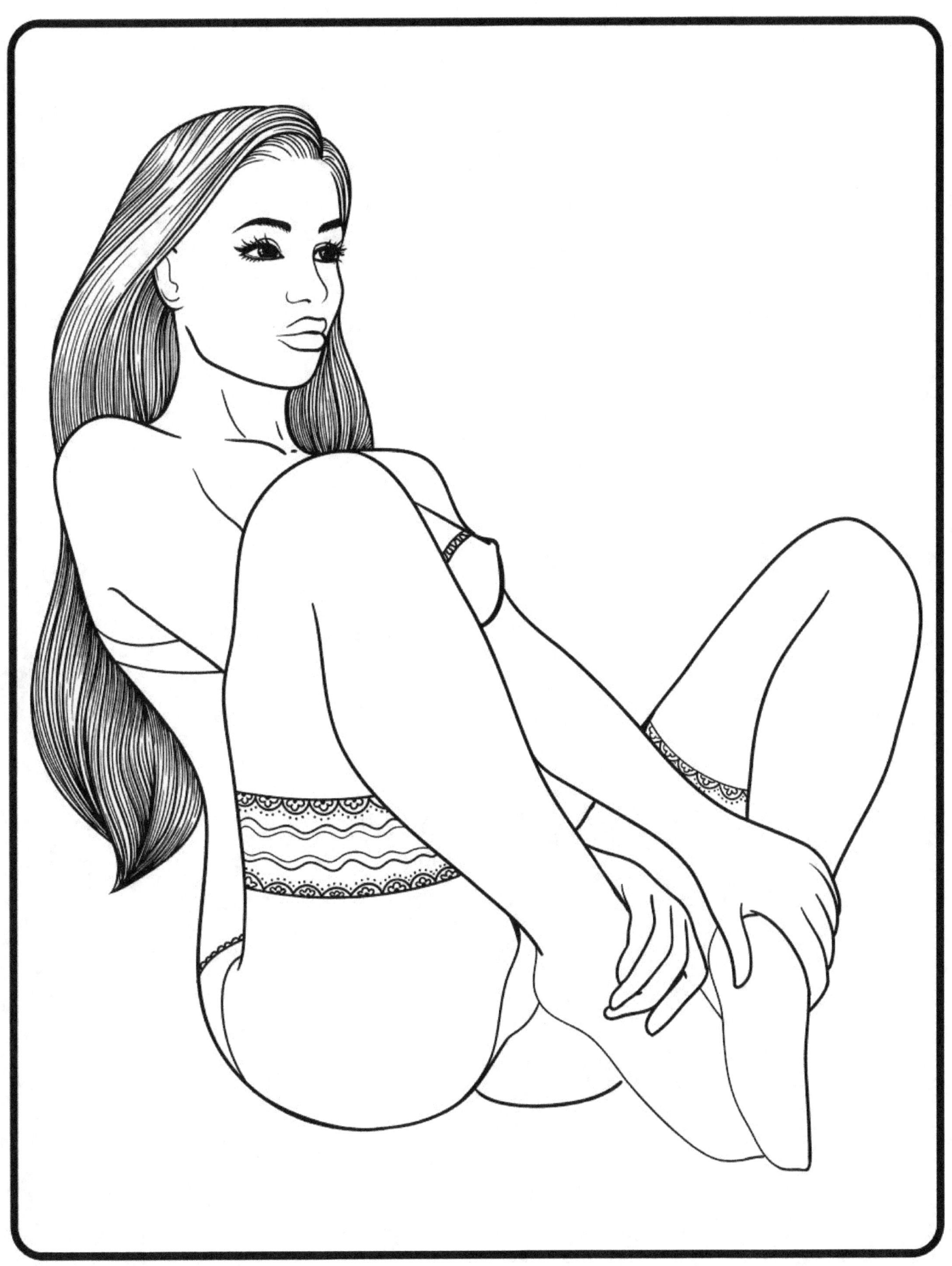

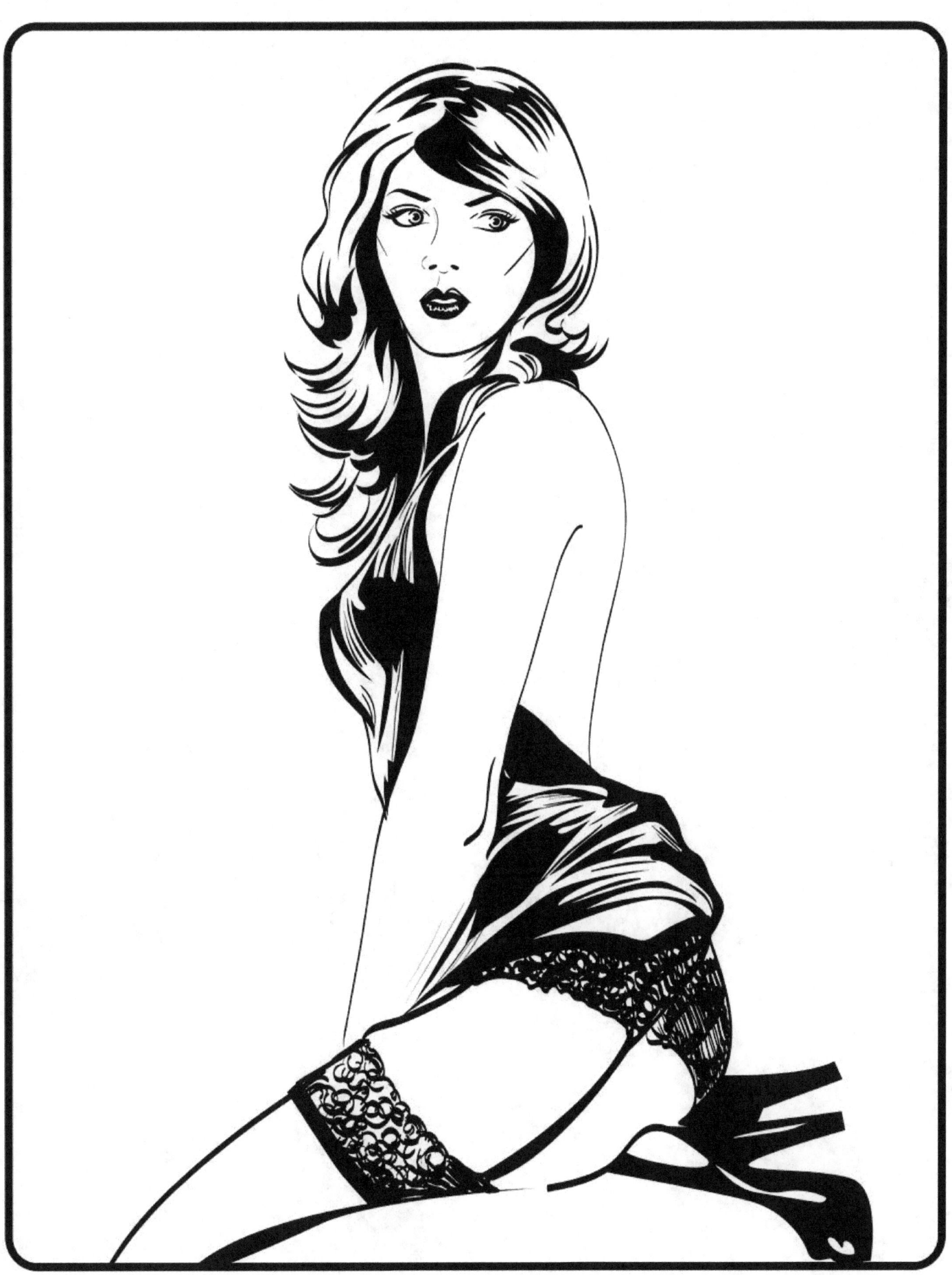

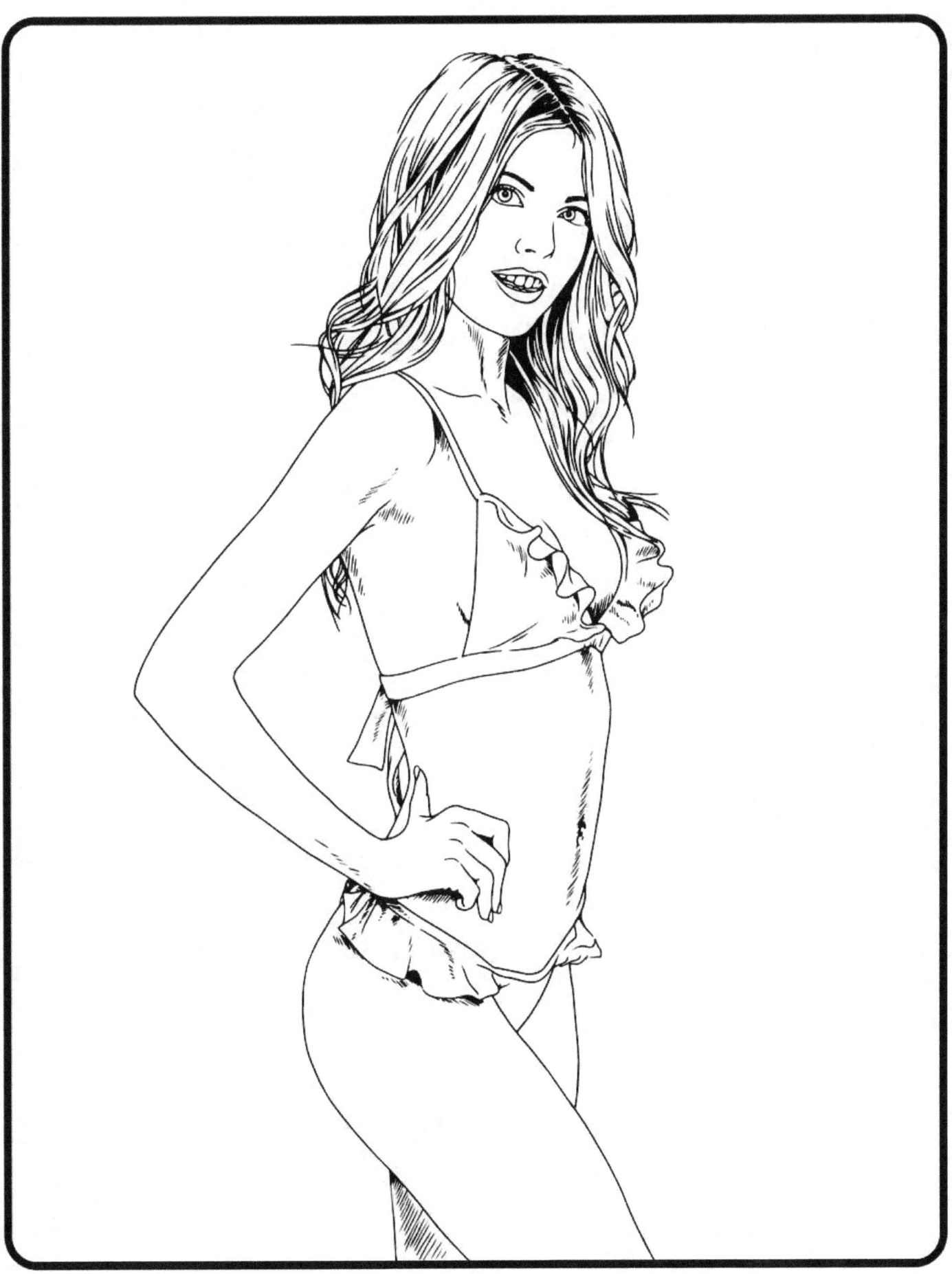

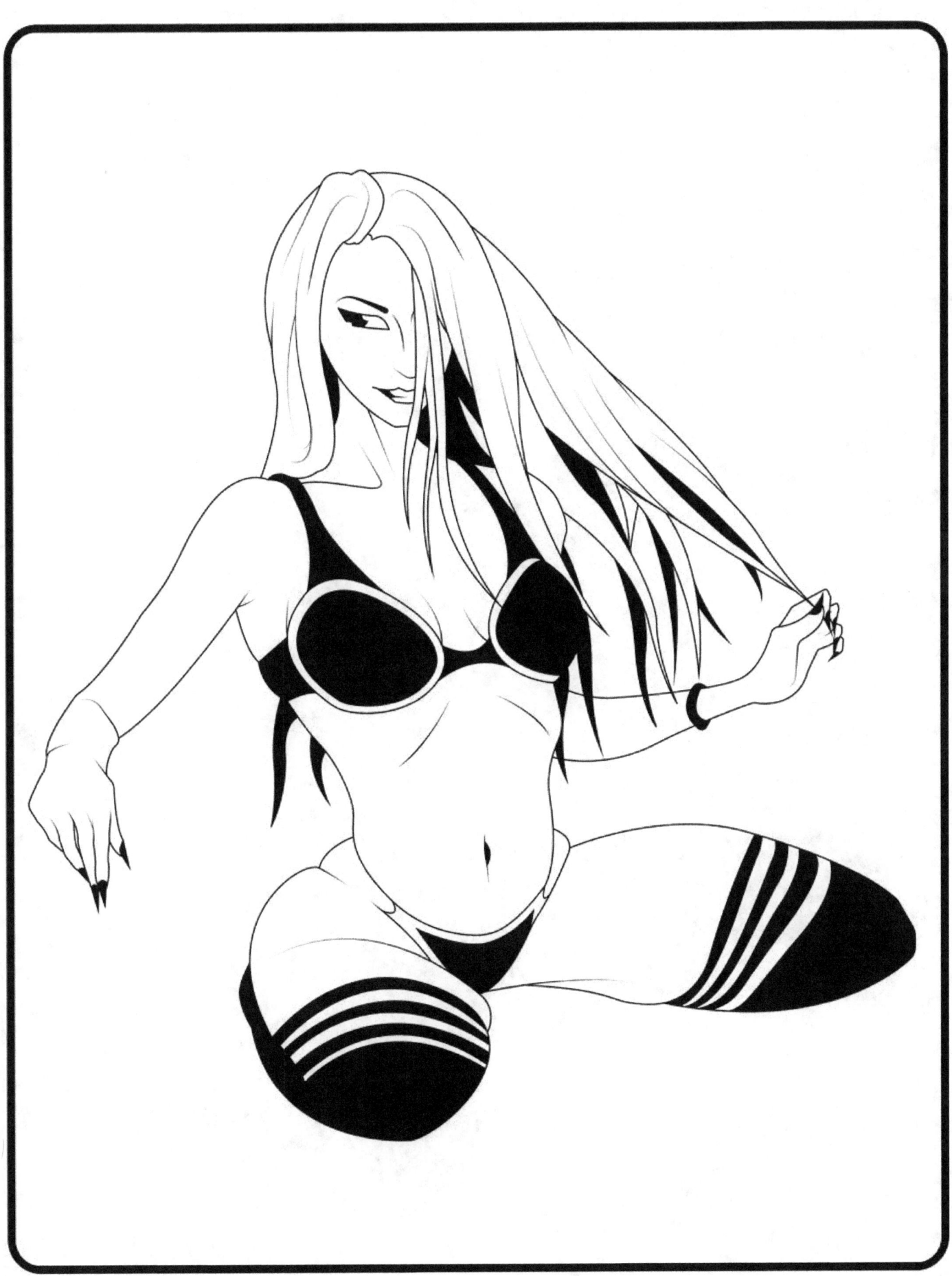

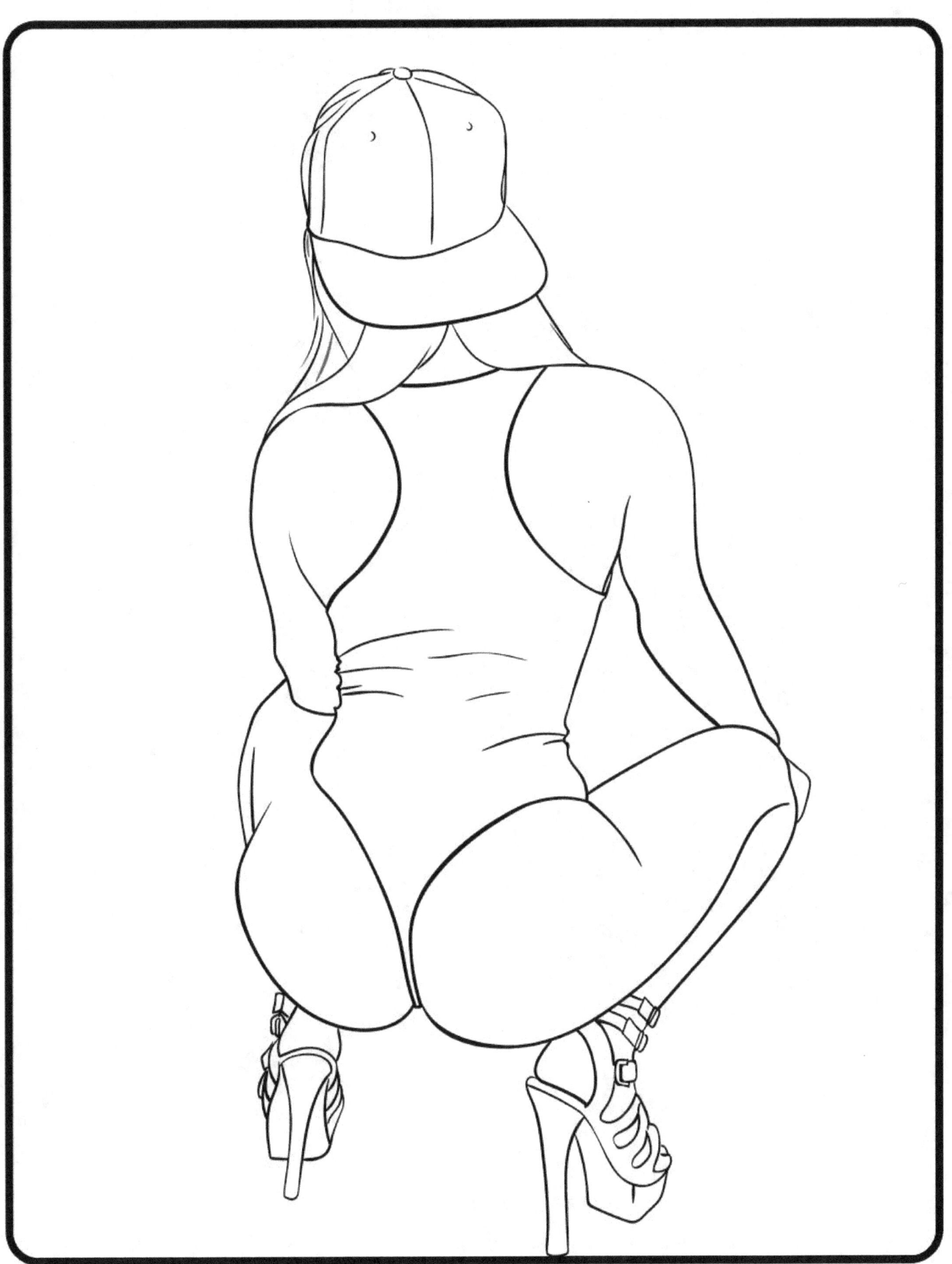

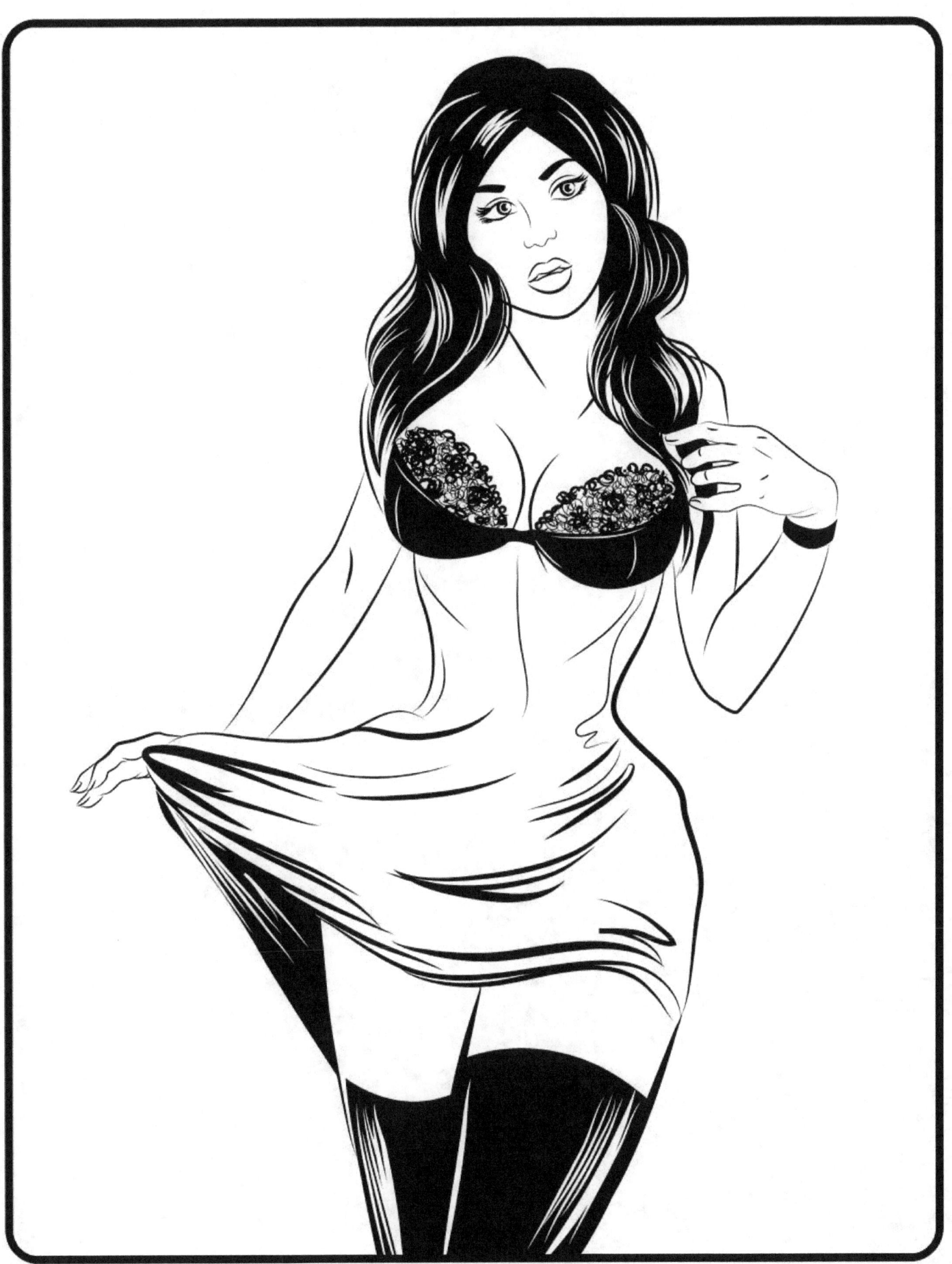

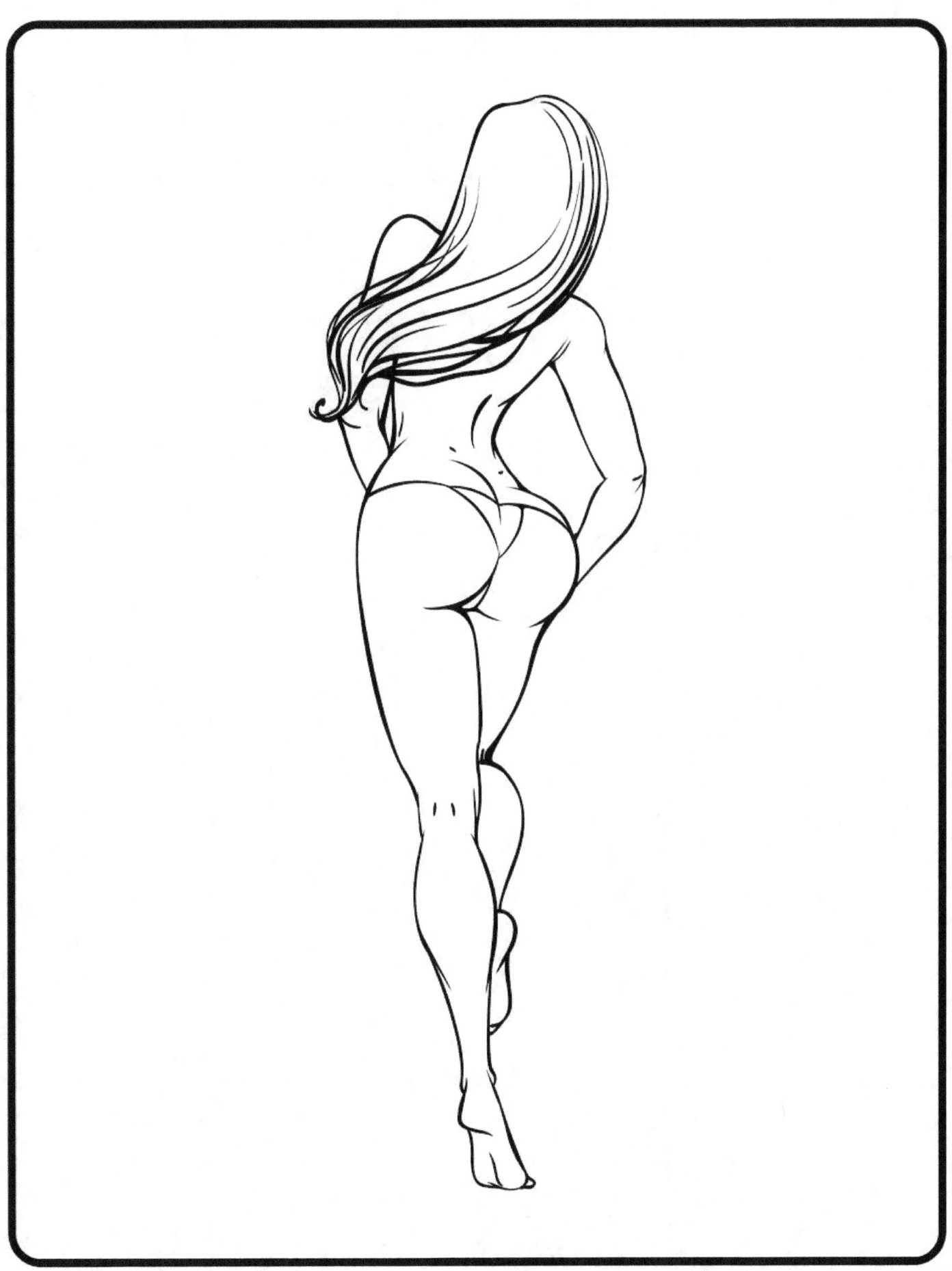

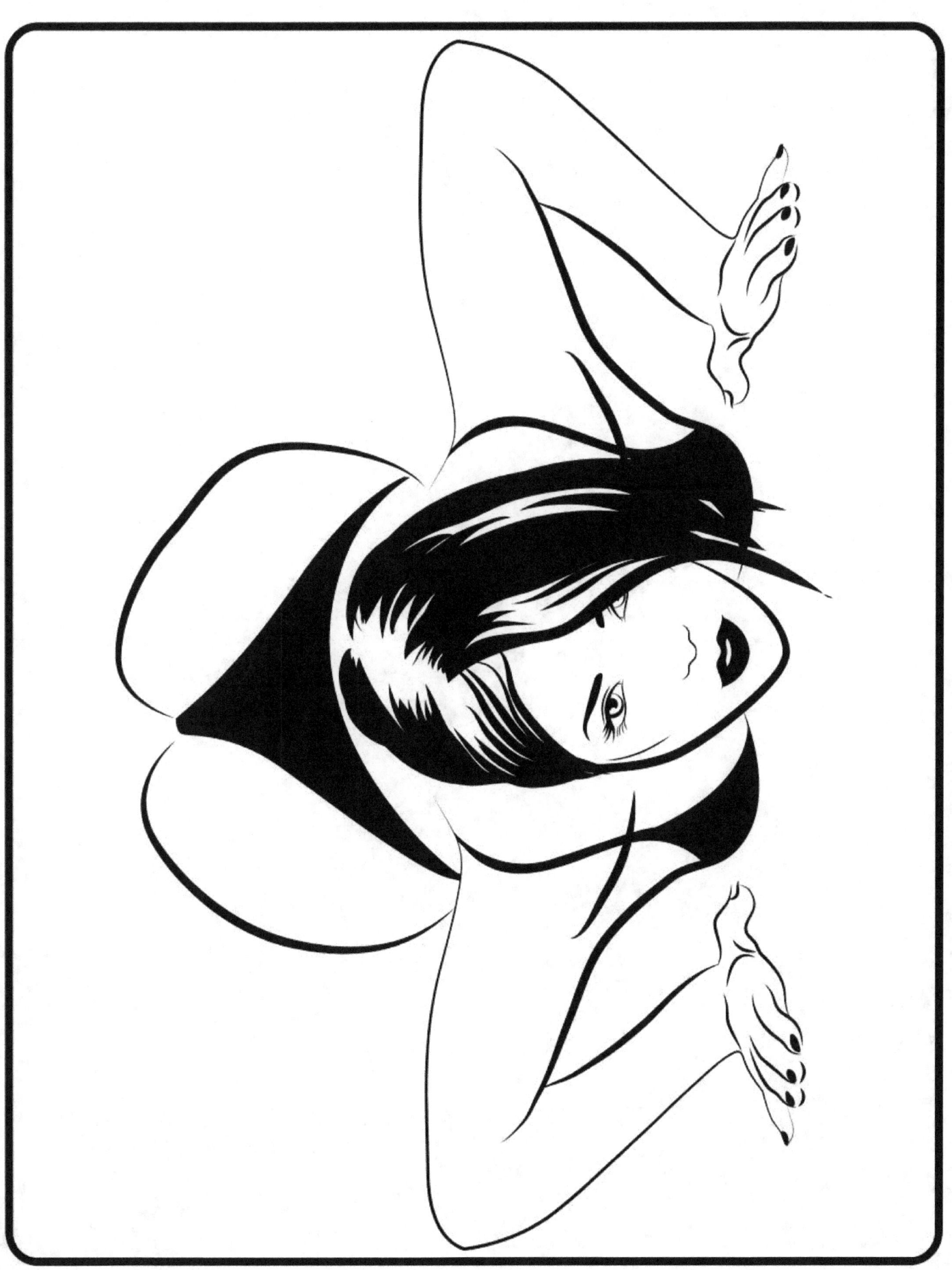

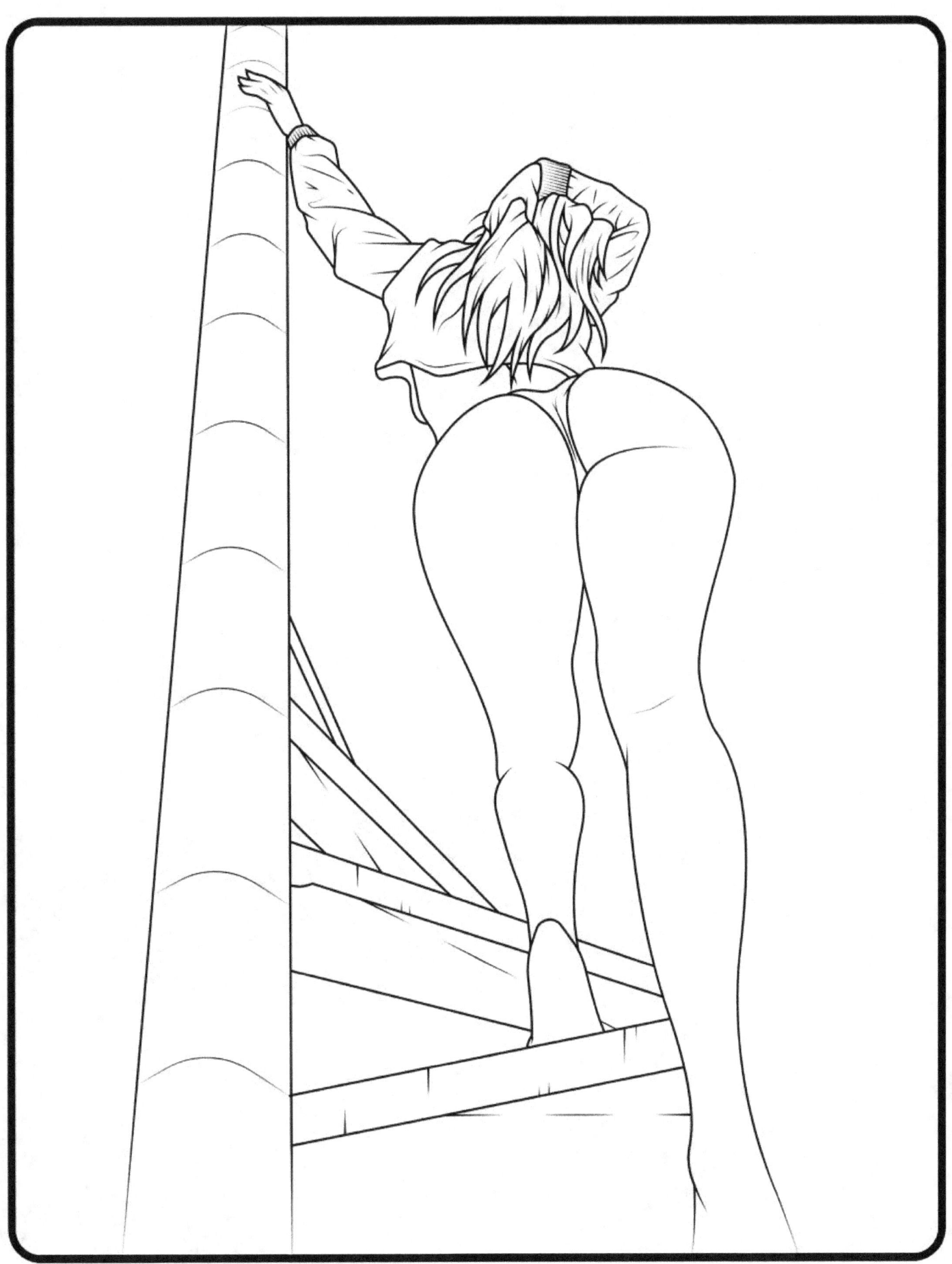

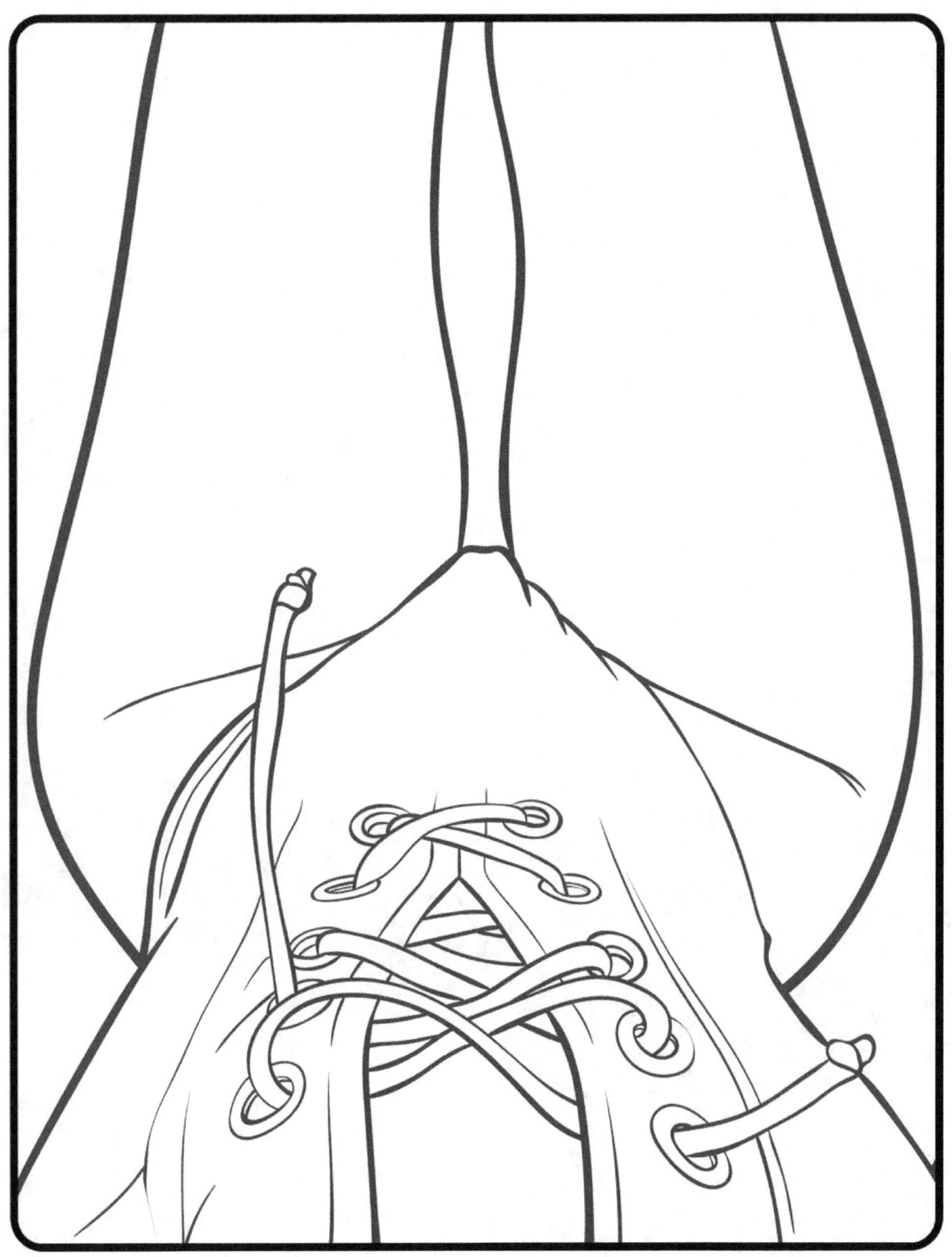

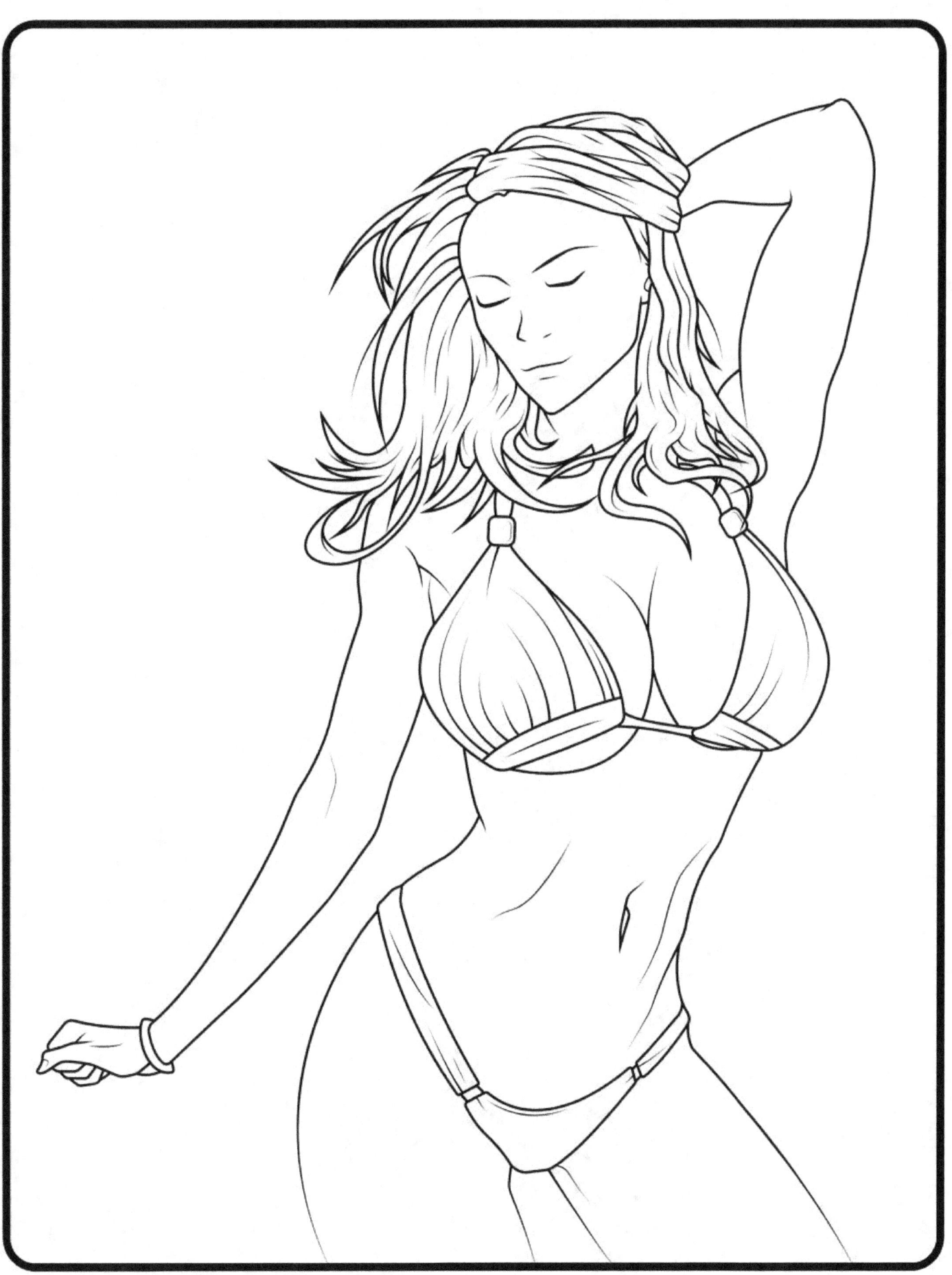

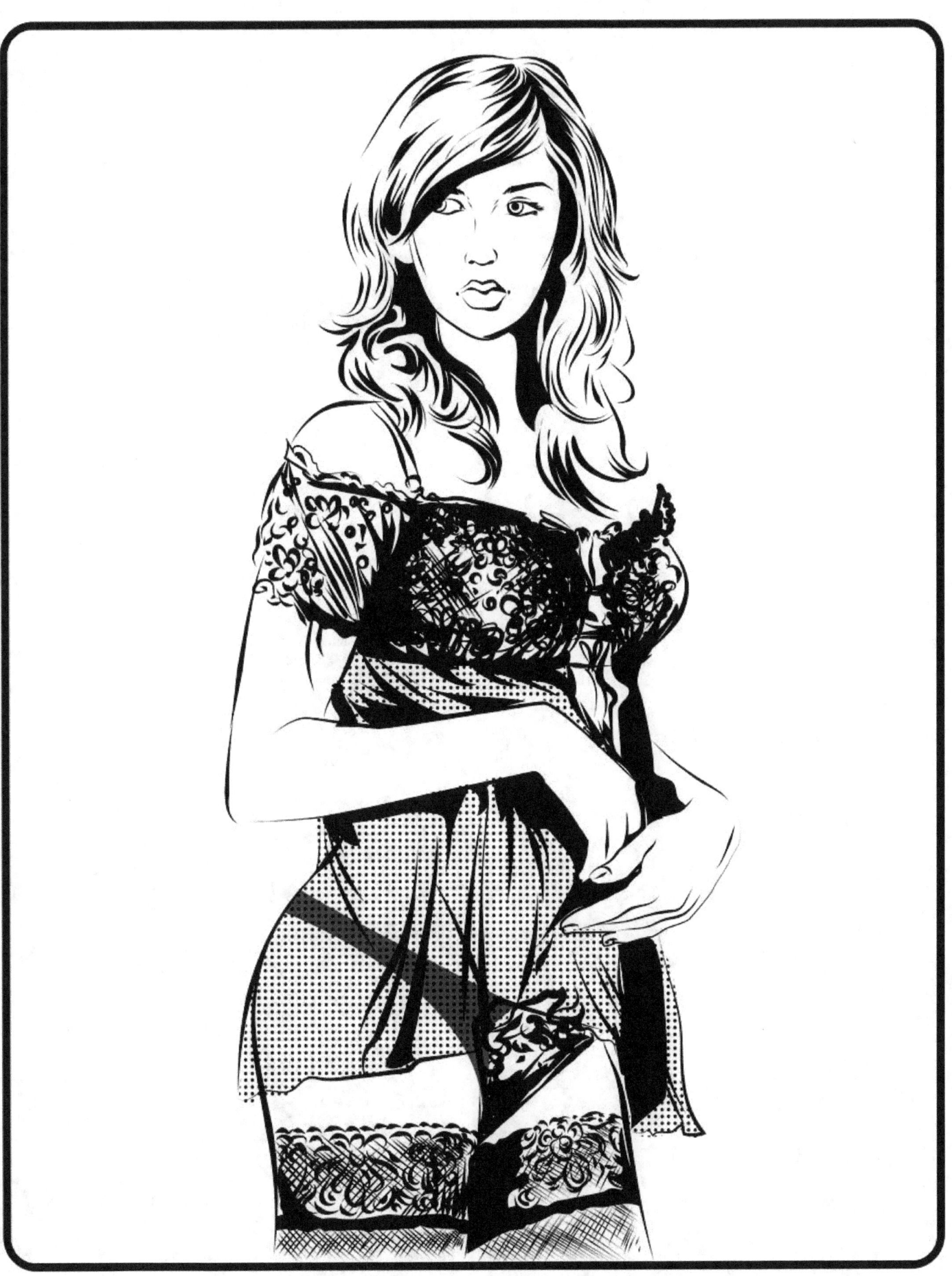

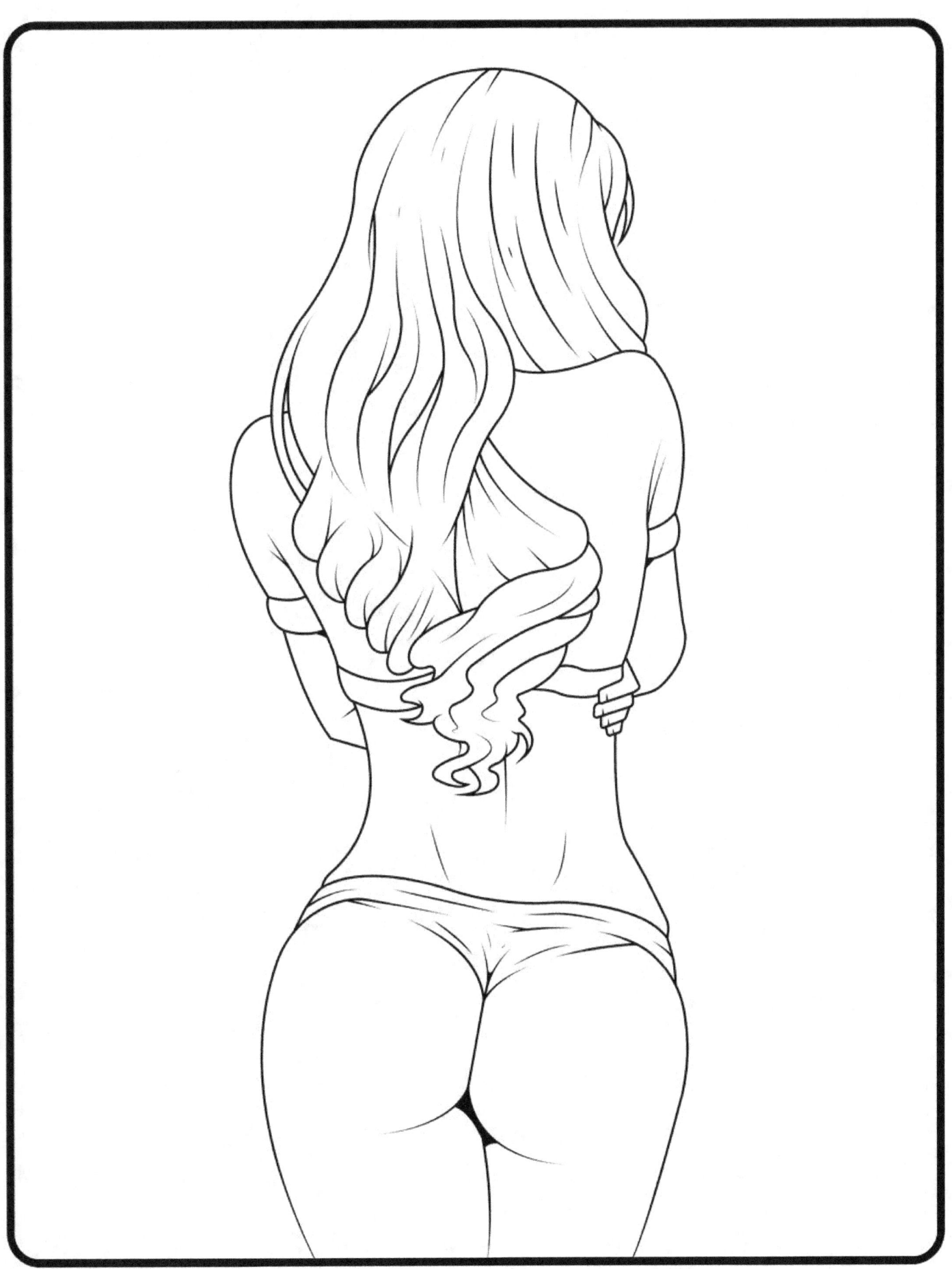

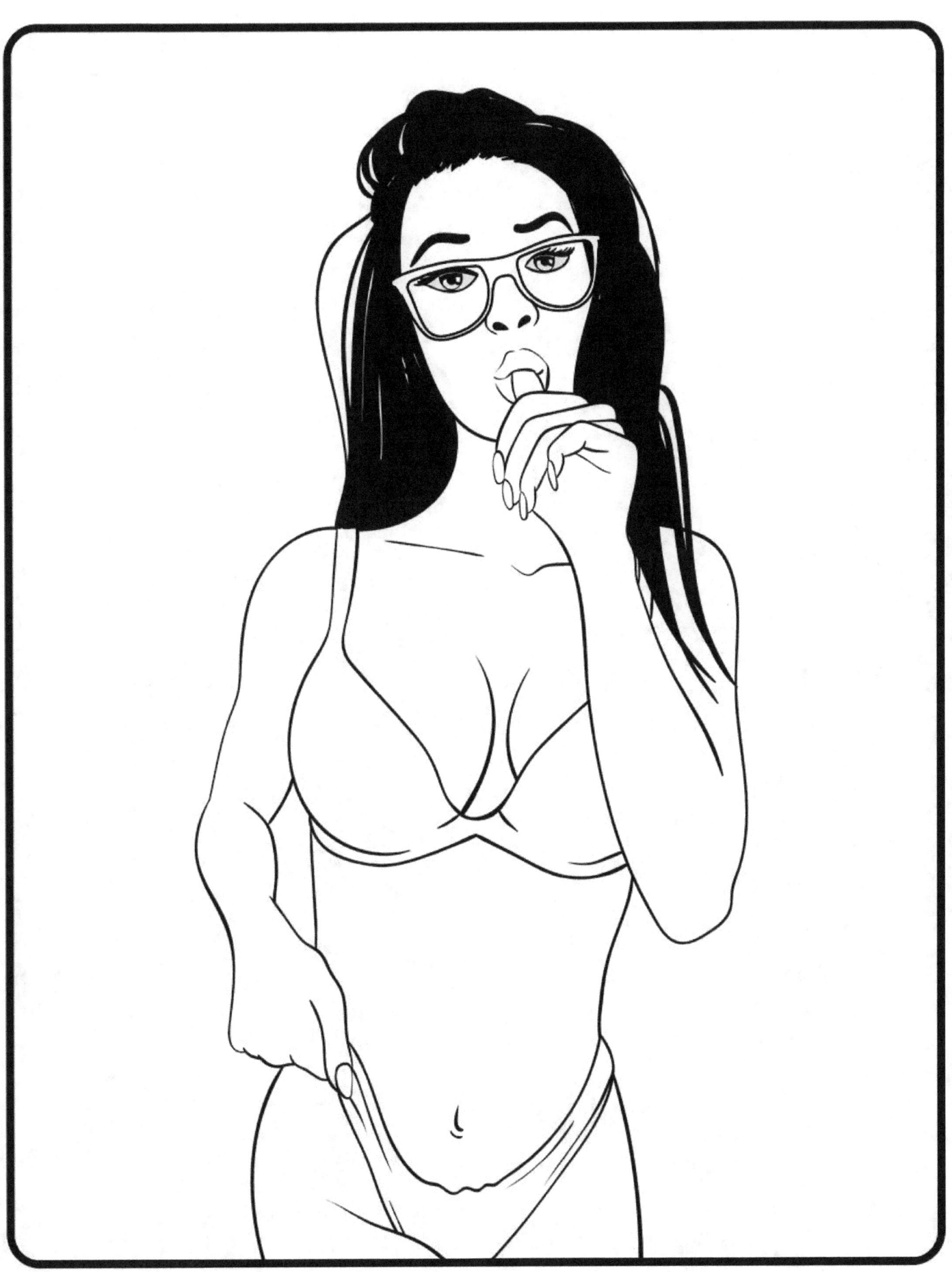

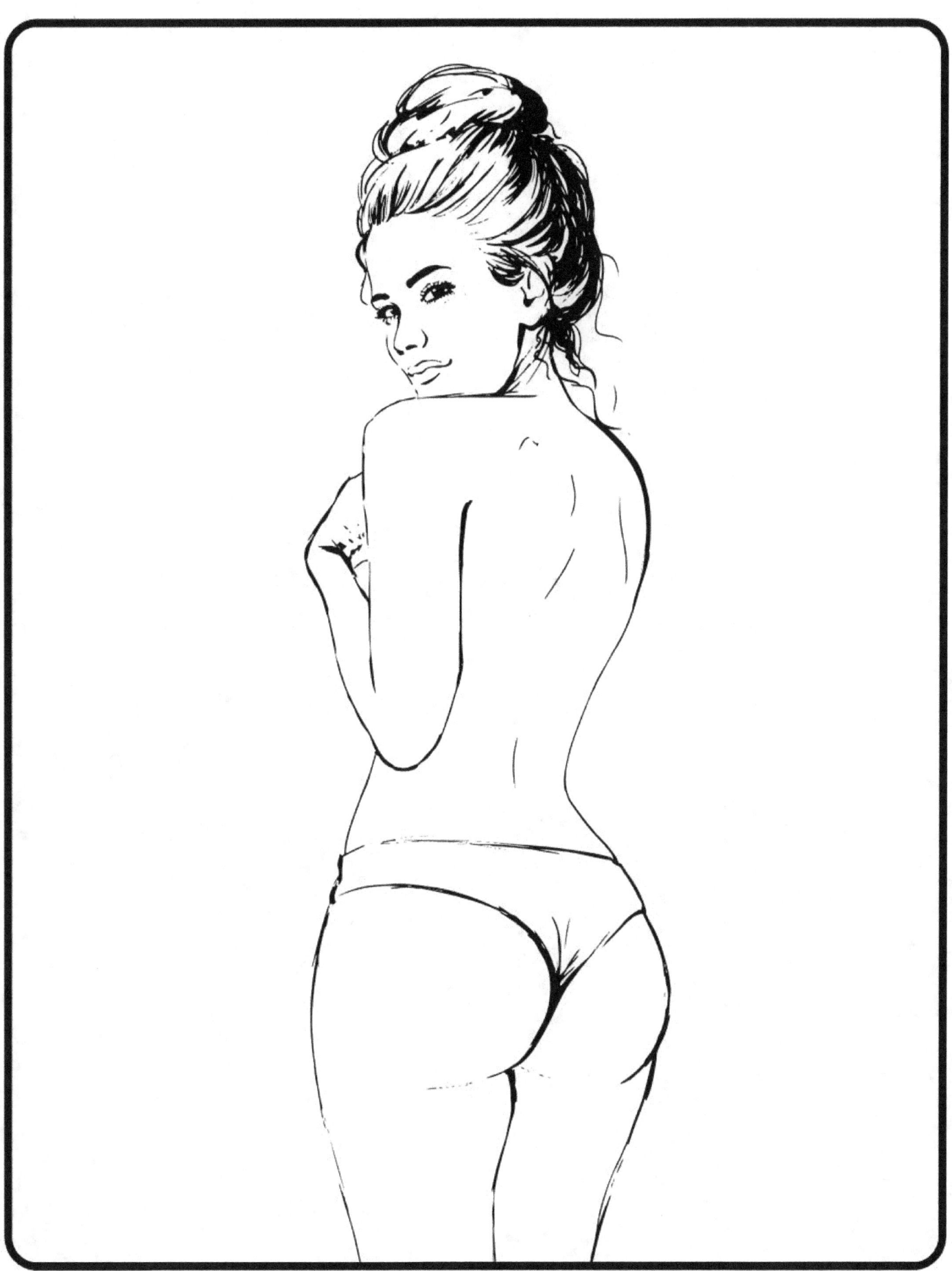

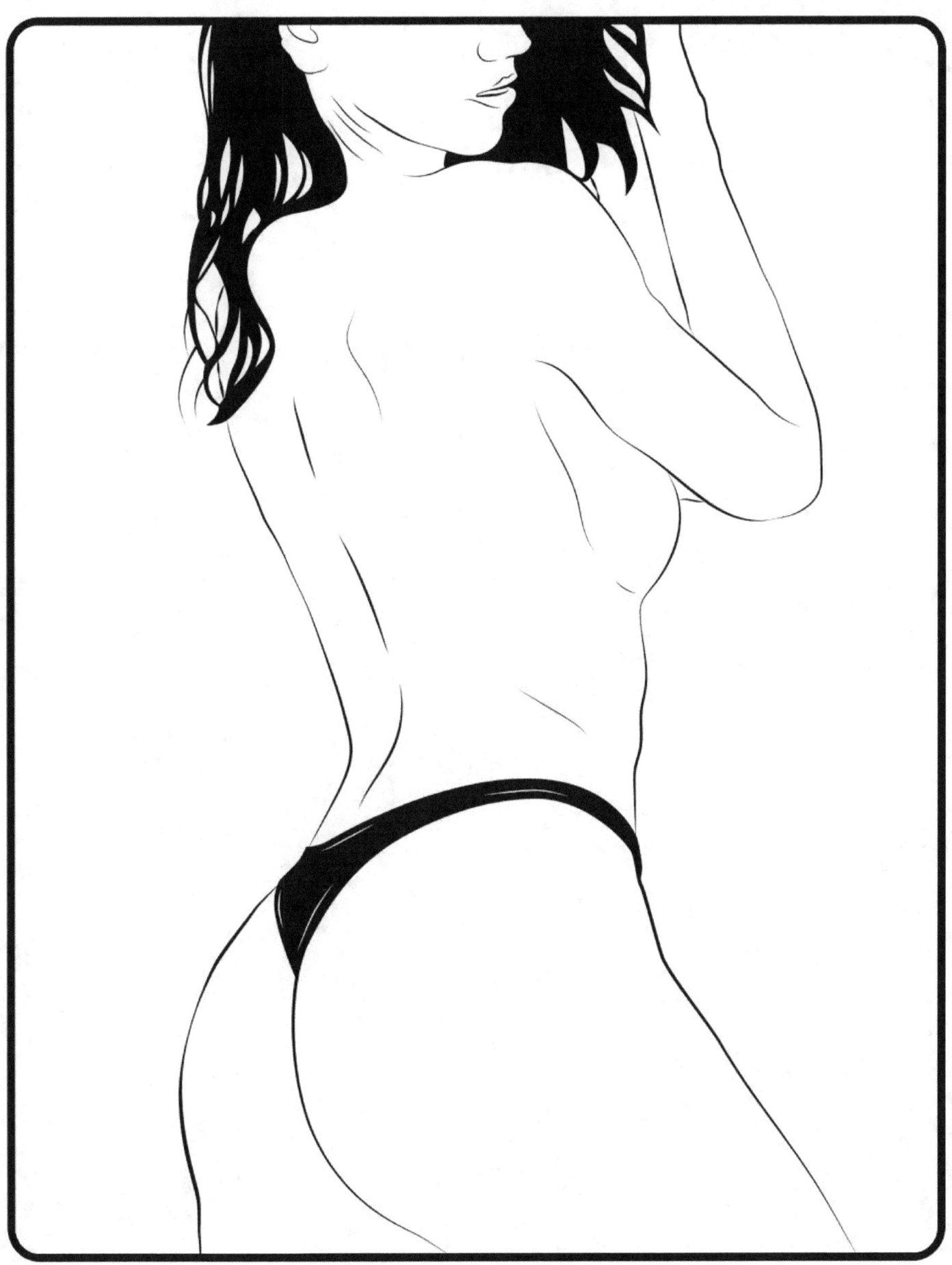

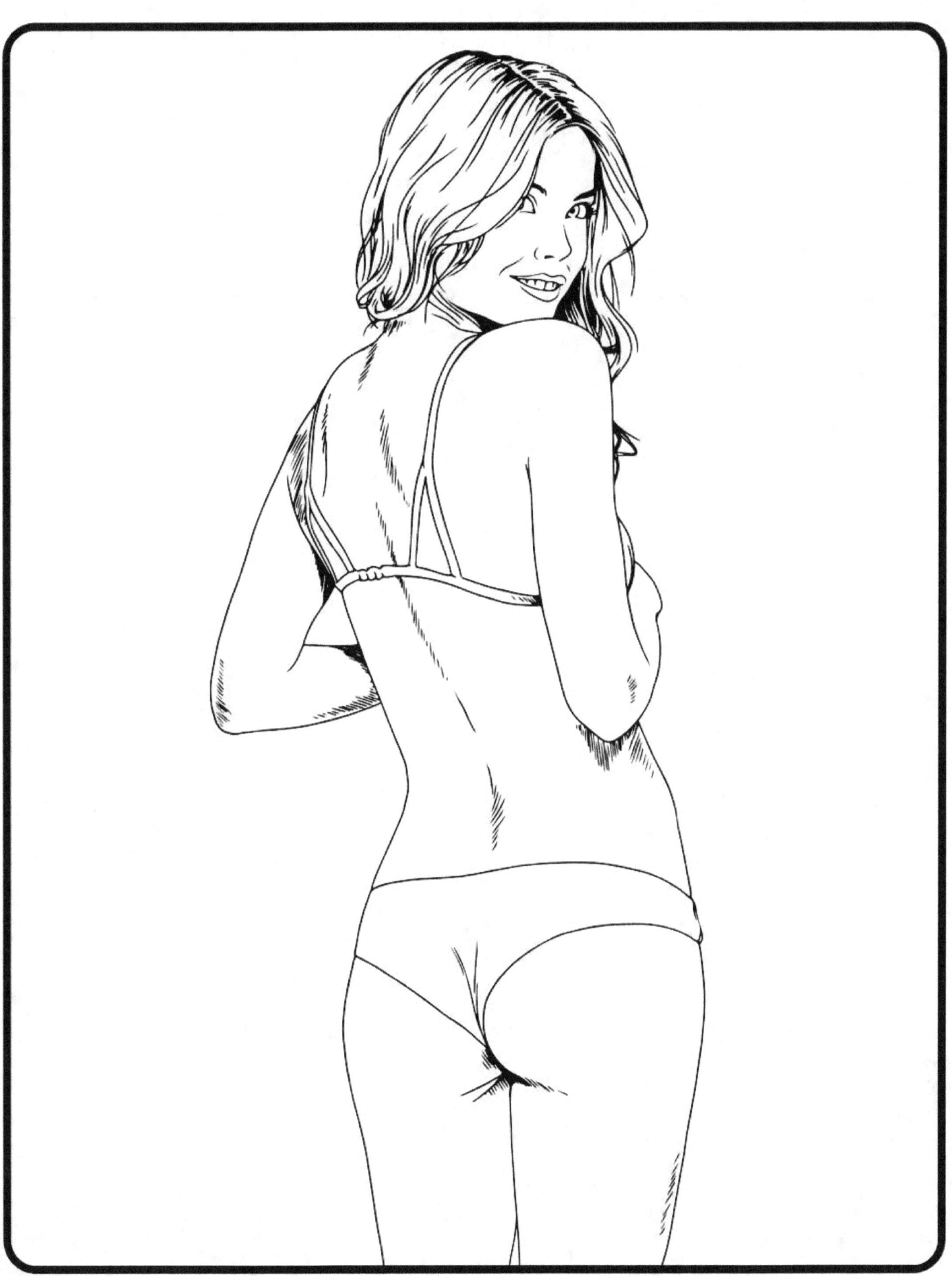

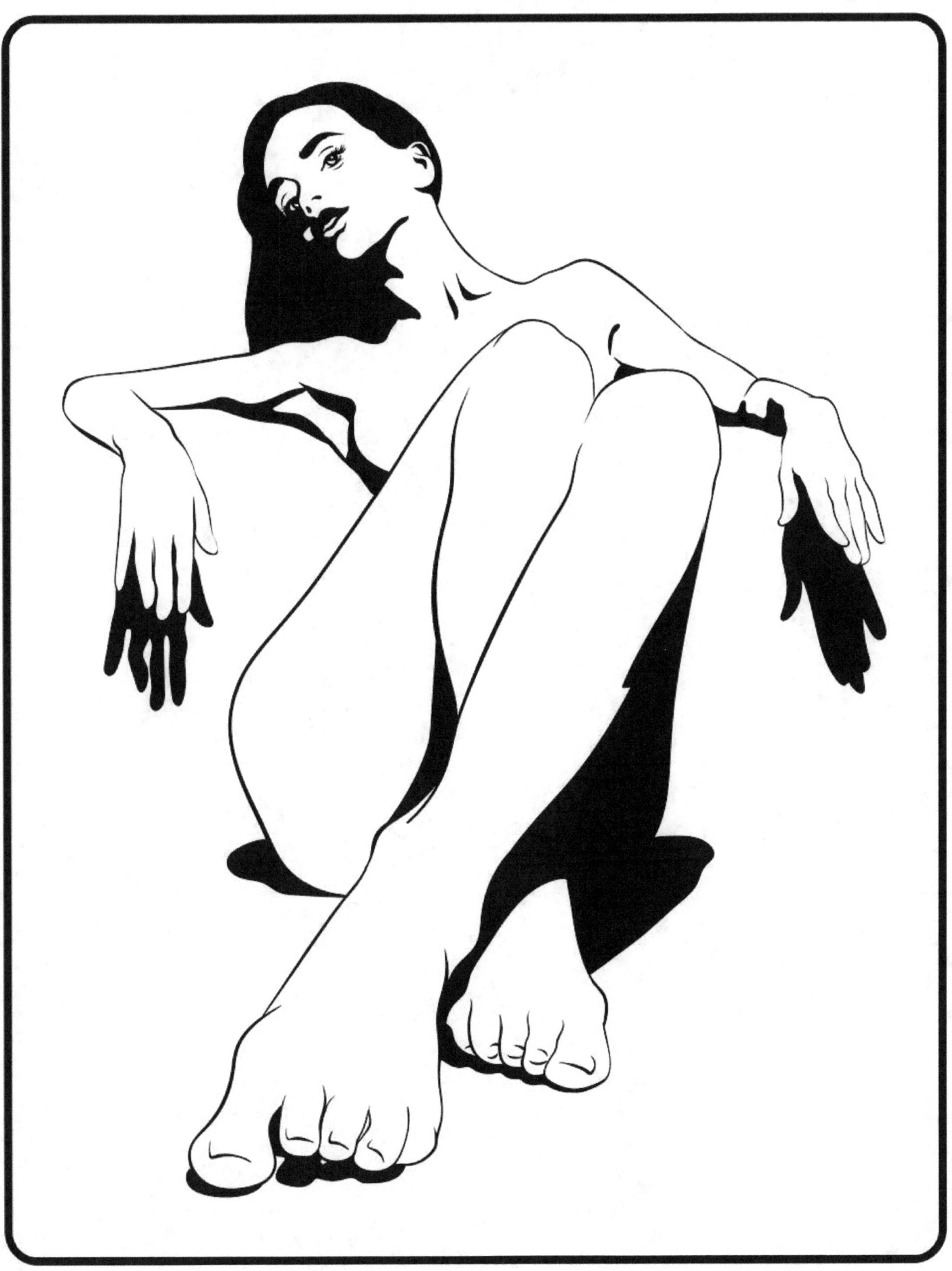

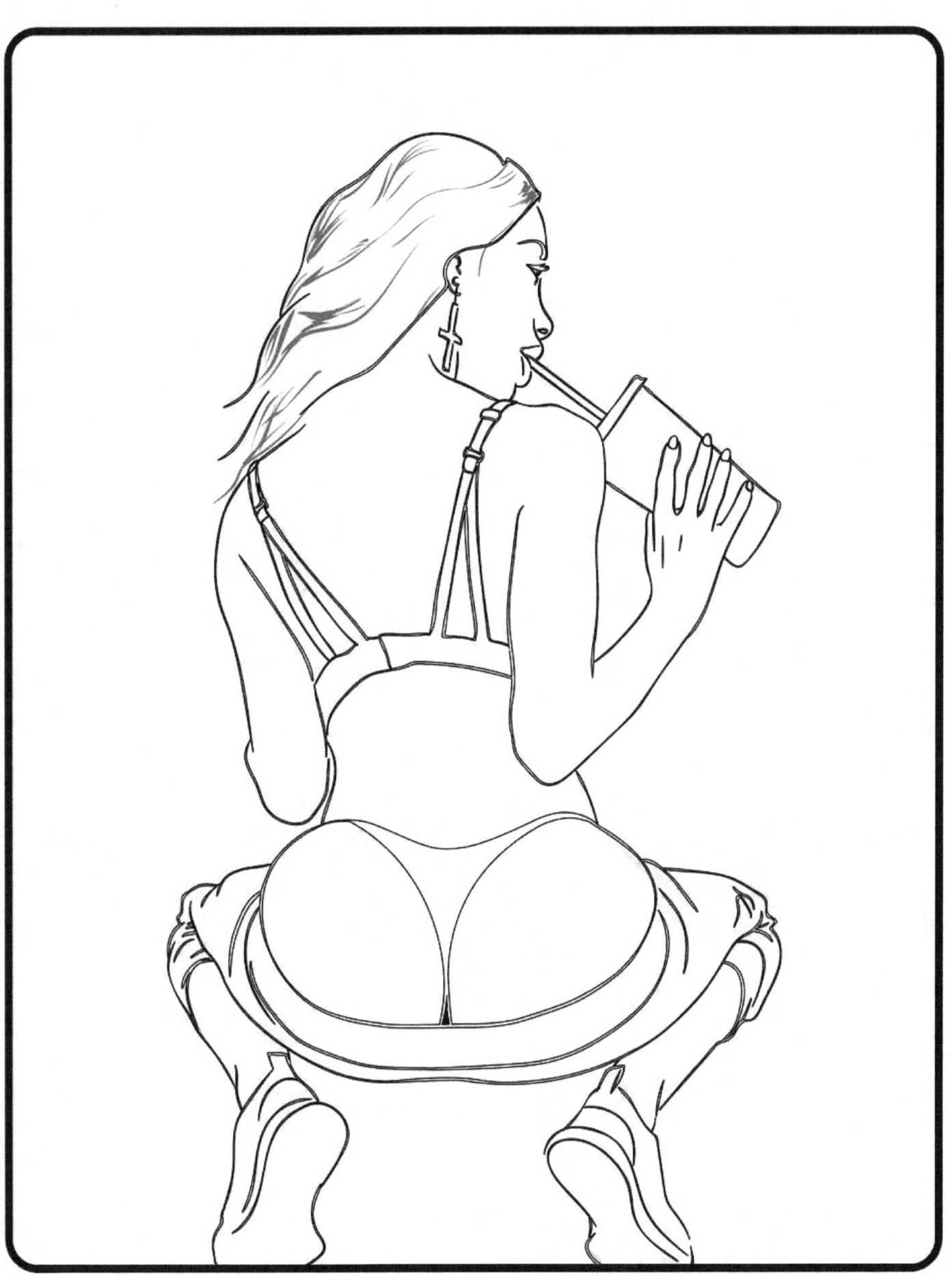

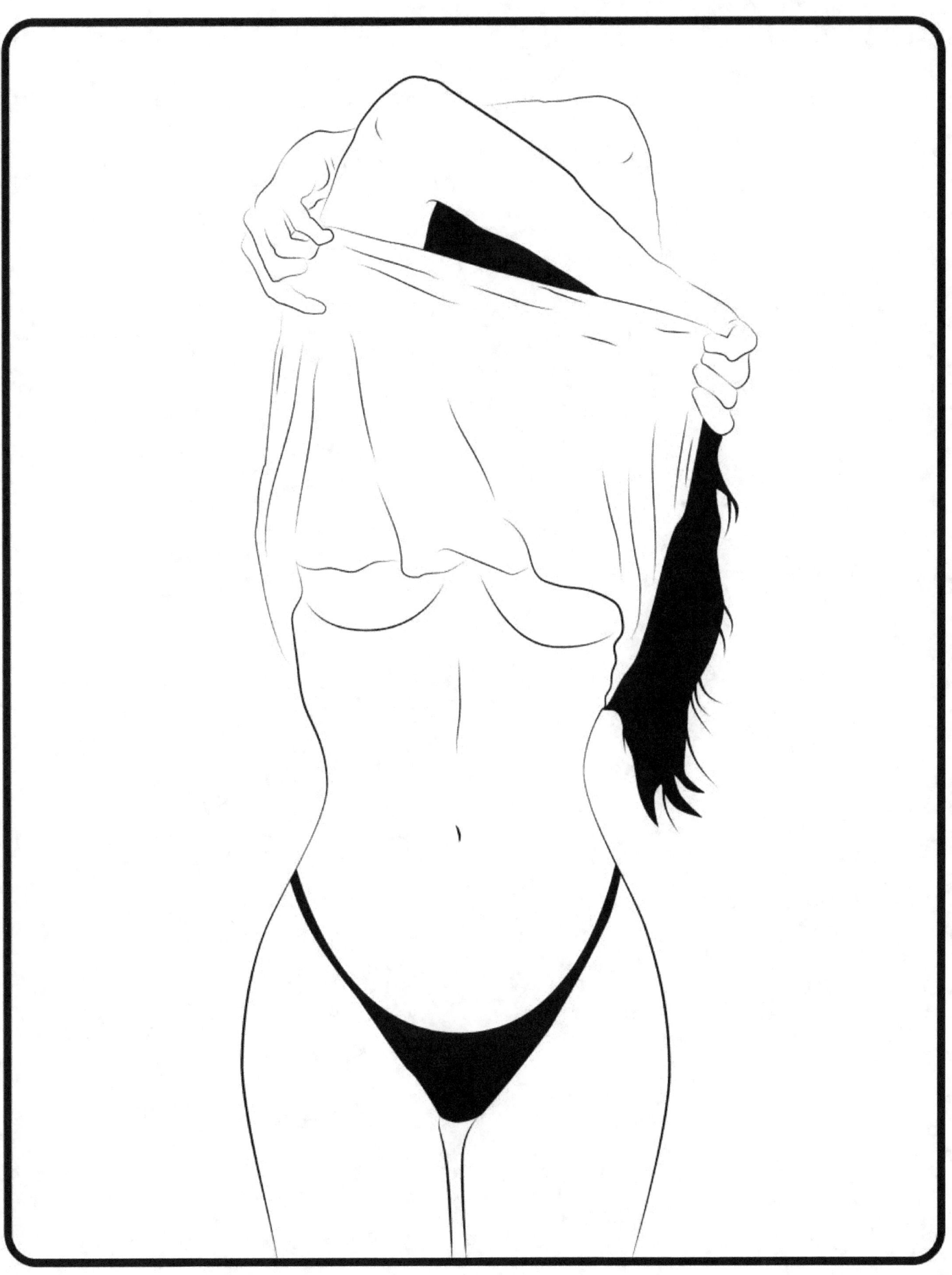

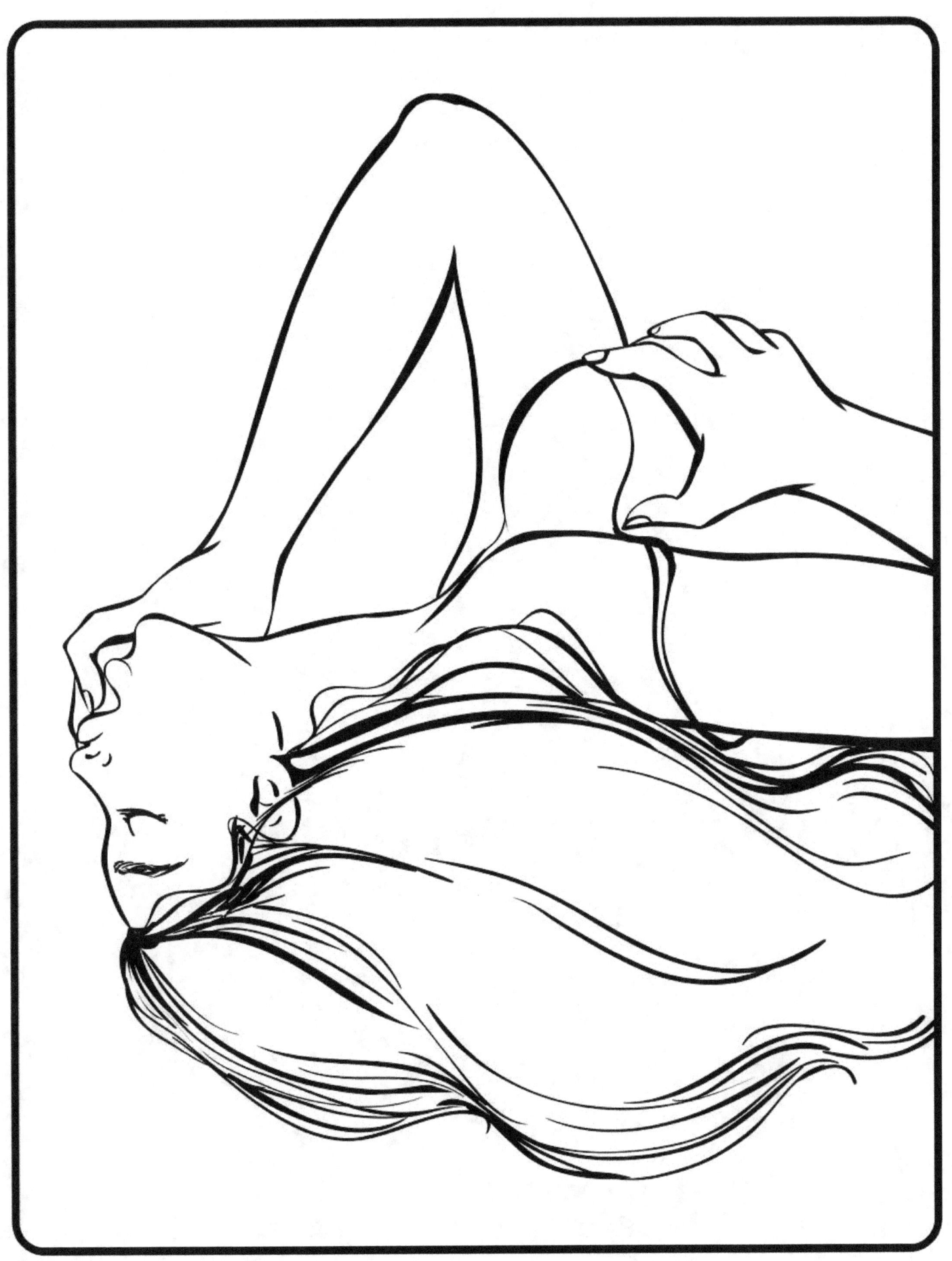

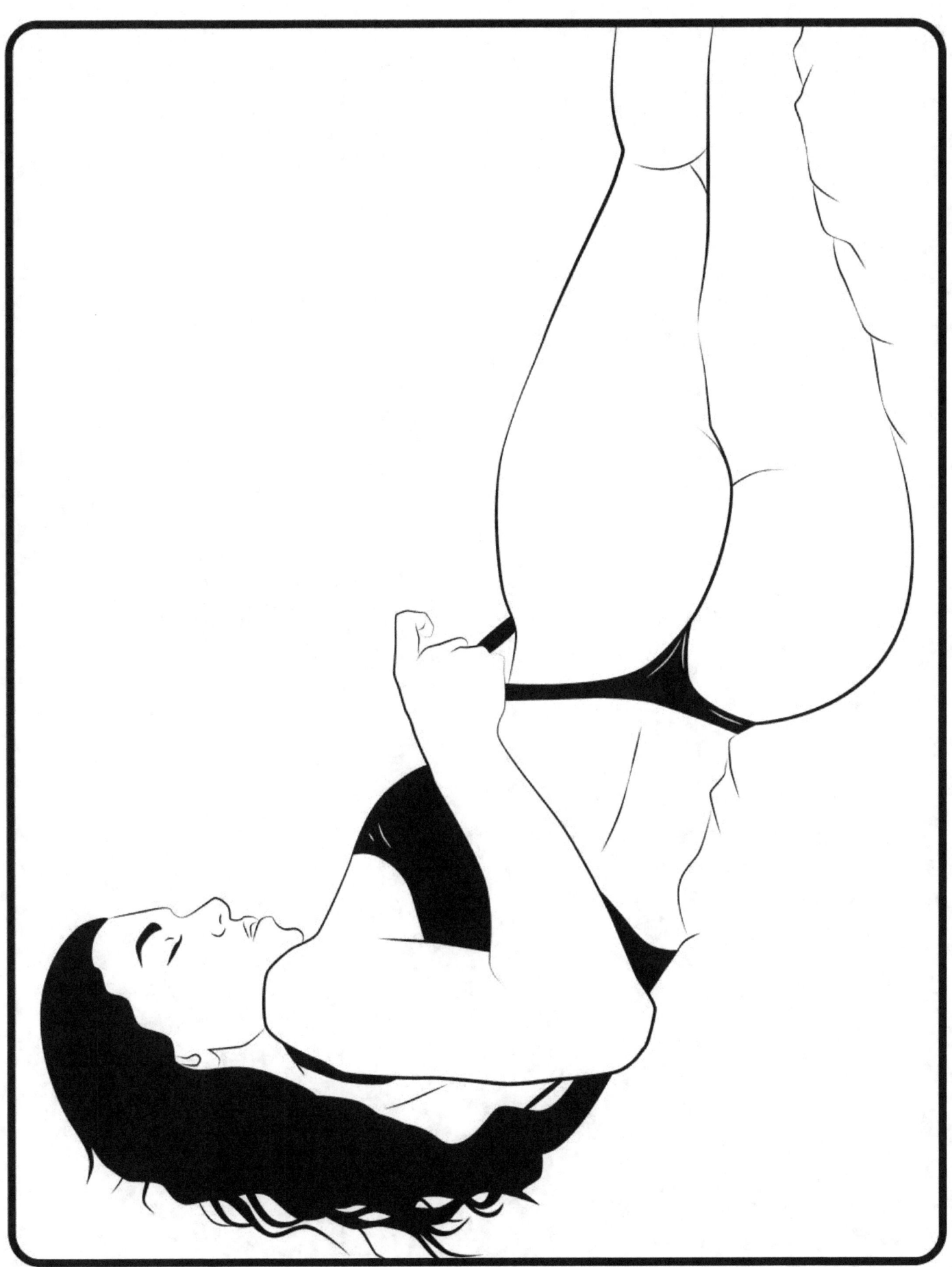

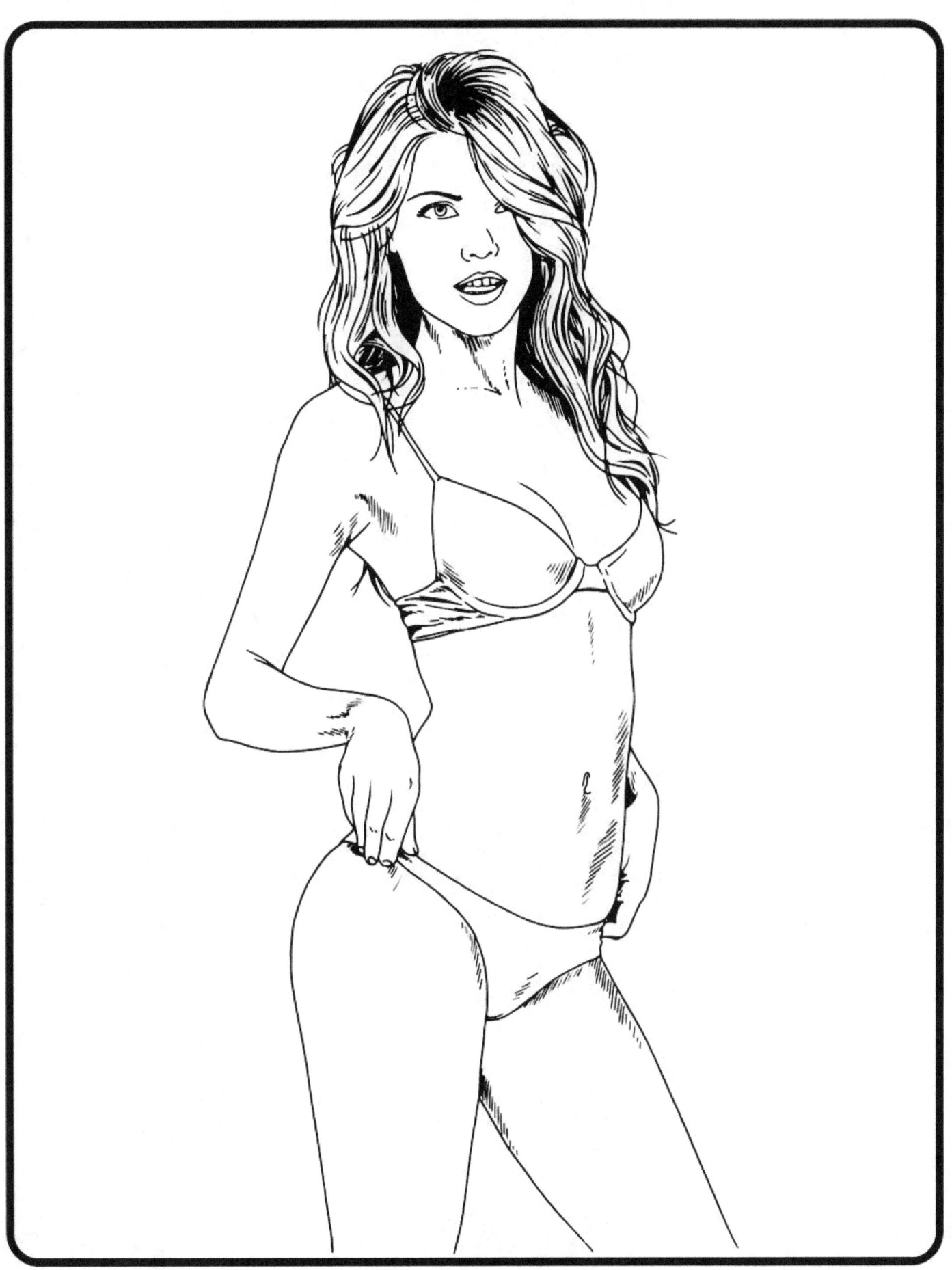

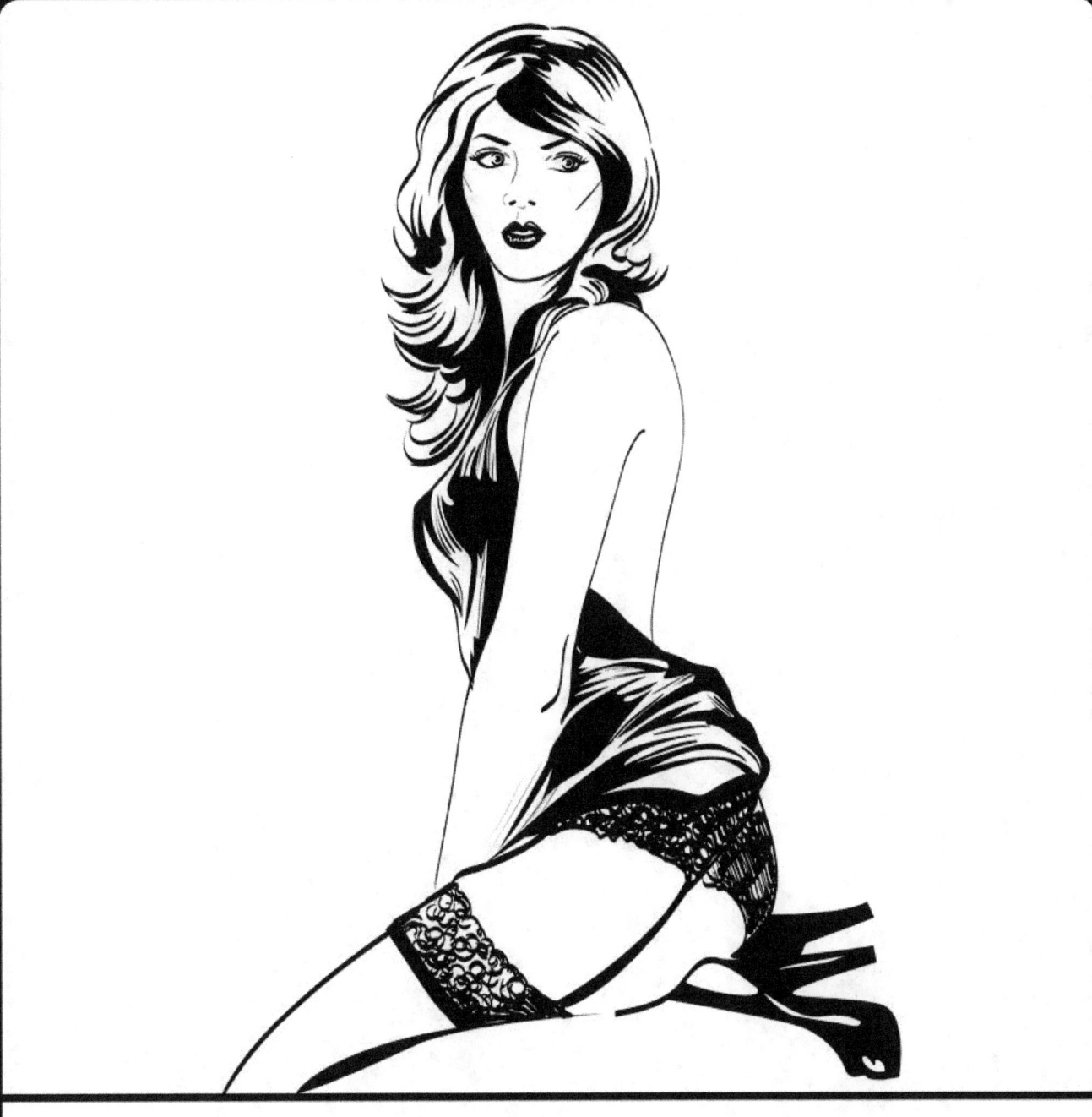

Thank you for buying this book

If you like the book, please consider leaving a review,
it will help author to create better books in the future

www.amazon.com/Katrin-Stark
www.amazon.co.uk/Katrin-Stark

www.ingramcontent.com/pod-product-compliance
Lightning Source LLC
Chambersburg PA
CBHW080527220526
45465CB00006B/2618